D1247663

The Simple Guide to
Rebreather Diving

*Includes both semi-closed circuit and
fully closed circuit systems*

BEST PUBLISHING COMPANY

The Simple Guide to
Rebreather Diving

*Includes both semi-closed circuit and
fully closed circuit systems*

By
Steven M. Barsky
Mark Thurlow
Mike Ward

BEST PUBLISHING COMPANY

ISBN: 0-941332-65-9
Library of Congress catalog card number: 97-077520

Composed, printed and bound in the United States of America.

Best Publishing Company
2355 North Steves Boulevard
P.O. Box 30100
Flagstaff, Arizona 86003-0100 USA

BEFORE YOU READ THIS BOOK...

Before you read this book, you must understand that we have made the following assumptions regarding the readers of this book:

1) You have a good understanding of the concept of partial pressures.
2) You are either a certified nitrox or mixed-gas diver.
3) You are taking, or will be taking, a rebreather course for the rebreather you intend to use.
4) You understand the risks in diving, and realize that there are special risks unique to rebreather diving.

IN MEMORIAM

This book is dedicated to the memory of Rob Palmer, an outstanding diver and a wonderful person.

Rob was among the world's foremost underwater explorers and diving instructors. His expertise included cave diving, the organization of underwater expeditions, underwater film-

Photo courtesy of Stephanie Schwabe.

making, and rebreathers. He also led numerous trips to the Blue Hole of the Bahamas and helped start a foundation, with his wife marine biologist Stephanie Schwabe, for the preservation and scientific exploration of these unique underwater formations.

A prolific writer and photographer, Rob wrote numerous books and articles to help educate divers. He wrote one of the first manuals for training recreational divers in the use of rebreather technology and one of the first books to clearly explain technical diving. He also wrote a book on his exploration of the Blue Hole.

Rob had a dry, understated wit that always made him a pleasure to be around. I never heard him speak ill of anyone and he was always willing to share his knowledge and experience.

Rob Palmer gave many people their first introduction to rebreather diving. As an instructor, he was patient and thorough. He was also exceptionally generous and open with his time. He is sorely missed.

Steve Barsky
January 1998

ACKNOWLEDGEMENTS

Rebreathers are not complex pieces of equipment, but because there are so many different types of systems, putting a book together on the topic turned out to be a complex job. Like so many topics in diving, there is no one person who knows everything about rebreathers, which made us rely upon the kindness of many people to bring this work to completion.

First and foremost, we would like to thank Jim Joiner, our publisher, who supported the concept for this book from its inception. Jim saw us through many difficult moments and always had a kind word for us.

Kristine Barsky modeled for many of the photos in the book, above and below the water. She also served as the principal grammar editor for the text and spent many hours reviewing the manuscript.

Tim Chapman of Ocean Technology Systems made available their Buddy Phone® wireless communications system to assist our shooting.

Bob Christensen, former commercial diver, UDT diver, and commercial diving instructor, took the time to read the text and provide critical comments to help improve our work.

Mark Conlin provided several excellent photos from his rebreather adventures with Howard Hall and Bob Cranston. Mark's underwater experiences span the globe and his photography is first rate.

Dave Cowgill shot photos for us at NEDU to illustrate the Navy's rebreather testing capabilities.

Howard Hall shared his personal experiences in rebreather diving based upon his many expeditions for underwater filmmaking. Howard also permitted us to accompany him to shoot photos during his first test dives with his new IMAX camera housing at the Coronado Islands near San Diego.

Mike Harris, marine biologist with the California Dept. of Fish and Game, graciously allowed us to use his photo of Christine Pattison from the Department's sea otter recovery team operations.

Diving legend Hans Hass provided us with a memorable historical photo of himself and his wife, Lotte, from their early days of rebreather diving. Dr. Hass was writing books and shooting films several years before Jacques Cousteau made his mark on the world of diving.

Nick Icorn kindly allowed us to photograph several historical rebreathers from his extensive collection of antique diving equipment. Nick's collection of dive gear is renowned around the world.

Mike Iswalt of Bio-Marine Instruments supplied us with technical information and a historical perspective on their closed circuit systems.

Dave Junker, retired Navy master chief, was the Unmanned Test Officer for life support apparatus at the Navy Experimental Diving Unit (NEDU) for many years. Dave reviewed the manuscript and helped us with numerous comments and suggestions to improve our work. We couldn't have completed this book without Dave's help and insights. Dave also shot the photo of Mike Ward used with his biography in the back of the book.

Avi Klapfer, underwater photographer, liveabord dive operator, and rebreather diver allowed us to use several of his great photos of Mark Thurlow in action.

Gary Long of W.R. Grace Co., assisted us with technical information and specifications regarding Sodasorb CO_2 absorbent. The Sodasorb Manual, published by W.R. Grace is an invaluable reference.

Linda Longnaker of Best Publishing did the layout for the book and helped us with the technical details of publishing.

Dr. Michelle Miller, Ph.D. in immunology and infectious diseases, explained the details of disinfecting life support systems to us.

Geri Murphy of Skin Diver Magazine provided us with one of the photos of Rob Palmer used in the front of the book. Geri's photos have appeared in Skin Diver for many years and her work is outstanding.

Clark Presswood, retired Navy SEAL commander, shared technical information on the testing of military rebreathers.

Christian Schult of Dräger supplied us with technical information and photographs from their archives. Kirstin Denker of Dräger also located technical and historical information for us and was always ready to help. Russ Orlowsky of Drager Safety in Pittsburgh, Pennsylvania, also supplied technical information and assistance on Dräger products.

Stephanie Schwabe, wife of the late Rob Palmer, made available one of the photos of Rob used in the front of the book. She is the director of the Rob Palmer Blue Hole Foundation based in the Bahamas.

Peter Jackson contributed his wealth of knowledge on the Fleuss Mask. Stephen James of North Safety Products/Siebe Gorman & Co. Ltd. helped secure permission for us to use early photos of the Fleuss for the historical section of the book. Leslie Leaney of the Historical Diving Society USA also helped in securing information on the history of rebreathers.

Bev Morgan assisted us with historical information and photographs of Navy rebreather systems. Bev also reviewed portions of the text for technical accuracy. Bev's friendship and support are things we treasure.

Connie Morgan who manages the archives for her father, Bev Morgan, helped locate several photos we needed and made sure we got them on time.

Peter Readey and his wife Sharron provided us with drawings and photos of their unique Prism Topaz rebreather. Peter is one of the leading authorities on rebreather technology. John Gunstream also provided technical advice regarding the Prism Topaz.

Pete Ryan helped us during the development of the Morgan M-15 full face mask. Pete was instrumental in the development of this mask and has always been there for us when we needed assistance.

Leon Scamahorn, instructor for Bio-Marine rebreathers, gave technical advice on Bio-Marine rebreather systems.

Without the support of all of the people mentioned here, this book would be much less than it turned out to be. Many thanks to all of you.

Steve Barsky, Mark Thurlow, Mike Ward

INTRODUCTION

Although I was a commercial diver for many years and did saturation diving to depths in excess of 500 feet, I was thoroughly intimidated when I went to Nassau to take a rebreather diving course from Rob Palmer in the summer of 1996. I understood mixed gasses, having made and run numerous mixed gas and saturation dives. I had even done gas mixing and cleaned systems for oxygen use. I had written numerous manuals for commercial diving helmets and techniques and I had made many dives with prototype full face masks and helmets.

Yet as I boarded the plane at the start of my trip, I felt as though I was about to get involved with a diving activity that would be very complicated. What if I didn't understand it? What if the skills were beyond my capabilities? What if I made a fool of myself and was unable to successfully complete the course?

Upon arriving in Nassau, Rob Palmer took me through the intricacies of the rebreather in a very simple manner. I learned there was nothing particularly complicated about the equipment, that it was rugged, as well as easy to use and maintain.

I must also admit that when I first took the rebreather apart, aside from being astounded by its simplicity, I was surprised that we hadn't performed our set-up in a cleanroom environment. I had half expected that we would wear surgical gowns and masks and that everything had to be sterile.

In reality, although it is important to maintain a reasonable degree of cleanliness, and take the normal precautions you should take when handling oxygen enriched gas mixtures, assembling a rebreather requires little more precaution than what you would use when handling open circuit nitrox gear. You could probably have roaches crawling around inside the breathing bags of most rebreathers, while you were diving, and it wouldn't affect a thing – unless one of the critters ended up in your mouth!

Diving with a rebreather opened up a whole new level of enjoyment for me that I had not previously experienced. For the serious underwater photographer and small boat owner, the rebreather is the ultimate way to dive.

Originally, this book was to be a joint project between myself and Rob Palmer. We had been working on the book for several months when Rob disappeared during an open circuit dive in deep water in the Red Sea off the coast of Egypt. To say I was shocked and deeply saddened would be an understatement. Rob was a wonderful, kind person, and our growing friendship made me very happy.

Rob's death also put this book on hold, temporarily. I knew that I did not have the expertise to complete this book by myself, because like most subjects in diving, there is no one person who knows everything about it. However, I also knew that Rob would want to see the project brought to fruition.

One of the people I knew who had extensive experience with fully closed circuit rebreathers was Mark Thurlow. Mark is a highly experienced diver and has worked with Bob Cranston, Howard Hall, and Marty Snyderman using rebreathers on numerous underwater film projects. Mark has also worked extensively with Bio-Marine and made test dives with their very first BMR500 rebreather.

Mark joined me in the project only under the condition that we would make every effort to take the mystery out of rebreathers to make them accessible to the average diver. Since this was the same goal that Rob and I had agreed upon when we started the book I felt confident that I had made a good decision in bringing Mark aboard.

Mike Ward of Diving Systems International, and a former Navy diver, joined the project under the same conditions; i.e., that we debunk the myths of rebreather diving. Mike has a vast range of practical rebreather diving experience with both fully closed and semi-closed systems. Mike has done extensive work at the Navy Experimental Diving Unit (NEDU) and has written numerous manuals for Navy diving systems.

I feel that we have met the original goals of this project, to present the facts about rebreathers, as well as explaining how to use them in a simple, understandable fashion. I hope that you will find this book takes the mystery out of rebreathers and opens up a new type of diving for you.

Steve Barsky
Santa Barbara, California

TABLE OF CONTENTS

PAGE

Chapter 1 - Everything Old Is New Again 1

What is a Rebreather. 1
Types of Rebreathers. 2
Fully Closed Circuit Oxygen
    Rebreathers 3
Semi-Closed Circuit Rebreathers Using
    Pre-Mixed Gas. 7
Semi-Closed Circuit Rebreathers,
    Self-Mixing Systems 8
In the Beginning, there were Rebreathers. 11
The Future of Rebreathers 23

Chapter 2 - Applications for Rebreathers. 25

Advantages of Rebreathers 26
Gas Efficiency 27
Warm, Moist Breathing Gas 28
Silent, or Near Silent Operation 30
Optimum, or near Optimum Oxygen
    Partial Pressure 31
Disadvantages of Rebreathers 33
Rebreathers are Expensive 33
Rebreathers are not Light Weight 35
Cost to Operate. 36

PAGE

More Preparation to Dive 36

More Post-Dive Maintenance 37

More Complexity 38

Availability of Breathing Gas and
Absorbent Material 40

Applications for Rebreathers. 41

Chapter 3 - Common Elements of Rebreather Design 45

First Stage Regulator. 47

Carbon Dioxide (CO_2) Absorbents
Chemical Absorbents 48

Other Methods of Removing
Carbon Dioxide. 54

Scrubber Canister Design 55

Breathing Bag Design 58

Shroud. 62

Mouthpiece 63

Hoses. 64

Additional Considerations 65

Dealer Support 65

Which Rebreather Should You Buy? 65

Pre-Purchase Check List 67

Chapter 4 - The Hazards of Rebreather Diving 69

Oxygen Toxicity 70

Hypoxia. 75

Carbon Dioxide Poisoning 79

Asphyxia 82

Chemical Burns. 82
Extreme Decompression Commitments 84

Chapter 5 - Semi-Closed Circuit Rebreathers 85

How Mass Flow Semi-Closed Systems
    Work 86
Pre-Mixed Systems 86
Self-Mixing Systems 90
Rigging Your System for Diving 92
Pre-Dive Preparation 98
Gas Selection. 98
Gas Analysis 103
Packing the Scrubber Canister 103
Pre-Dive Assembly and Inspection 107
Testing Your Rebreather 109
Flow Testing 109
Negative Pressure Leak Test 113
Positive Pressure Leak Test. 115
Dive Planning 117
Calculating Your CNS
    Oxygen Exposure 117
Calculating Your Decompression
    Obligation 119
Donning Your Rebreather 122
Water Entry and Descent 126
During the Dive 127
Normal Ascents. 129
Emergency Procedures 131

Flooded Scrubber Canister 133
CO$_2$ Absorbent and Scrubber Failure 134
Breathing Bag or Hose Failure 134
Oxygen Sensor Failure 135
Post Dive Procedures 135
Maintenance and Storage 136

Chapter 6 - Fully Closed Circuit Electronic Rebreathers . . 139

The Next Step in Rebreather Evolution 139
How CCRS Work 142
Component Systems of CCRS 144
Inside the Breathing Loop 147
Advantages of Fully Closed Circuit
    Electronic Rebreathers 148
Rebreathers Look Cool! 151
Disadvantages of Fully Closed
    Circuit Rebreathers 151
CCRS Are Expensive 152
Training 153
Travel 155
Oxygen Logistics and Safety 156
No Bubbles, Some Trouble 156
Rigging Your System 157
Bail-Out Bottles 159
Pre-Dive Preparation 160
Gas Selection and Analysis 167
Planning a Dive 168
Donning a CCR 170

Entering the Water 171
In the Water 171
Buoyancy Control 174
Emergency Procedures 174
Failure to Turn the Rebreather On 174
Failure to Turn the Oxygen Supply On/
    Running Out of Oxygen 175
Loss of Diluent 175
Solenoid Failure 176
Battery Failure 177
Sensor Failure 178
Computer or Electronics Failure 178
Manual By-Pass Button Sticks Open 178
Absorbent Failure/CO_2 Buildup 179
Caustic Cocktails 180
Ascending at the End of Your Dive 181
Precautionary Decompression Stops or
    Actual Decompression 183
Semi-Closed Circuit Operation 184
Post Dive Maintenance 185

Chapter 7 - Rebreather Diving Accessories 189
    Full Face Masks 189
    Dive Computers 195
    Oxygen Analyzers 198

Chapter 8 - Is there a Rebreather in Your Future? 201
    If You Purchase a Rebreather 204

PAGE

About the Authors 207

           Steve Barsky 207

           Mark Thurlow 209

           Mike Ward 211

Glossary 213

Bibliography 217

Index 221

WARNING

Rebreathers offer a different mode of diving that is applicable to many diving activities. It is up to the individual user to decide when it is most appropriate to use a rebreather, or when another type of diving gear may be more suitable. Rebreathers are not the answer to every diving problem.

Diving with a rebreather presents more risks than diving with open circuit equipment. These risks include hypoxia, oxygen poisoning, carbon dioxide poisoning, and chemical burns, as well as all of the normal risks associated with open circuit scuba. If you are careless in using or maintaining a rebreather you may be seriously injured or even killed.

Every model of rebreather is unique. Just because you are qualified to use one particular type of rebreather does not mean that you are capable of using another model. You must be trained for each specific type of rebreather that you intend to use.

Proper training in using a rebreather includes both classroom training and practical experience in confined and open water, under the direct supervision of an instructor who is knowledge-able and experienced in rebreather diving. This book is not a substitute for rebreather training, but is intended to add supplemental information on rebreather diving.

How can you get close to wary creatures like hammerhead sharks? It's possible with a rebreather!

CHAPTER 1

EVERYTHING OLD IS NEW AGAIN

WHAT IS A REBREATHER?

Imagine yourself cruising along a beautiful tropical reef in the Sea of Cortez, swimming amidst a school of scalloped hammerhead sharks. The sharks pay no attention to you, as they cruise the reef. You look down at your depth gauge and see that you are at 60 feet and that according to the computer you are using you have another ninety minutes of bottom time before you even need to be concerned about decompression. You've already been underwater for almost thirty minutes, yet you're warm, comfortable, and have none of the "dry mouth" that normally starts to become noticeable during a long dive.

How can a dive like this be real? It's simple, if you are diving with a rebreather. With a fully closed circuit rebreather you have no bubble exhaust from your breathing system, you can make incredibly long dives without the need to decompress, and you are breathing warm, moist gas. The oxygen level in your breathing system is controlled by you, using the rebreather, so that you are breathing a mixture of gas that eliminates as much nitrogen as is safely possible from your gas supply.

Rebreathers are simply devices that capture and recirculate your exhaled breath, scrub out the carbon dioxide produced by your body, and add oxygen to replenish what you have consumed. They can be extremely efficient when used correctly and within their limits. With most rebreathers, you can make either one long dive, or several shorter dives, using gas cylinders that are dramatically smaller than the 80 cubic foot aluminum cylinders that most people presently use. The use of a fully closed circuit mixed gas rebreather will allow a person to dive to much greater depths and for longer times than conventional open circuit scuba.

When you dive with ordinary compressed air scuba, every time you take a breath you exhale most of the gas you have just inhaled into the water. This is quite wasteful since you don't use any of the nitrogen in the air and very little of the oxygen. The rebreather keeps recirculating the nitrogen (or other inert gas) and "making up" the oxygen to an optimal level. With the most efficient rebreathers, you can spend up to four hours or more underwater using two tiny cylinders of compressed breathing gas.

Today there are many different rebreather designs and new systems are constantly being developed. However, there are certain basic elements of rebreather design that are common to all rebreathers. These elements include one or more gas cylinders, a regulator (or regulators), one or more breathing bags, a carbon dioxide "scrubber", breathing hoses, and a mouthpiece. Every rebreather includes these basic components, although they may appear quite different from system to system. The design of these components will be covered in detail in Chapter 2.

TYPES OF REBREATHERS

Although all rebreathers contain the common elements that have already been mentioned, the design of these components varies widely from system to system and the way each system is assembled is quite different. Different engineers and designers have interpreted the basic requirements for a rebreather in ways that contrast dramatically with each other.

There are four fundamentally different types of rebreather systems. These include the following designs:

- Fully closed circuit oxygen rebreathers
- Fully closed circuit mixed gas rebreathers
- Semi-closed circuit rebreathers using pre-mixed gas
- Semi-closed circuit rebreathers that mix the breathing gas on board

Within these four categories of rebreathers there are tremendous variations of design and features from manufacturer to manufacturer. There are also subcategories that include whether the rebreather uses electronics to control the mixing of the breathing gas or whether it is done mechanically.

FULLY CLOSED CIRCUIT OXYGEN REBREATHERS

The fully closed circuit oxygen rebreather is the least versatile type of rebreather and is not generally recommended, used, or available for recreational or technical diving. This type of equipment was the original rebreather design and underwent extensive development during World War II. Since that time it has been refined and is still used by military divers around the world. In fact, oxygen rebreathers make up the majority of rebreathers used by military organizations worldwide.

The fully closed circuit oxygen rebreather is the most compact and lightest weight rebreather design on the market. Most systems use a single cylinder of pure oxygen and have a single breathing bag. These units typically provide a long bottom time, although today they are commonly limited to a depth of no more than 25 feet, with very short excursions to

40 or 50 feet under special circumstances. They emit no bubbles and are extremely simple to operate. Typically there are no electronics in these systems and they work strictly on a mechanical basis. Because these systems use pure oxygen they present serious hazards to the user and require close adherence to their depth limitations.

Oxygen rebreathers are ideal for clandestine military operations and this is their primary application. For this reason, their sales are strictly controlled and they are normally not available to the civilian population of most countries. They are also used by some police forces and by government agencies like the Central Intelligence Agency (CIA).

Closed circuit oxygen systems are relatively inexpensive to use since medical grade oxygen is readily available in most areas and no special mixing is required. Like all rebreathers, they require the use of a carbon dioxide absorbent chemical.

There are several models of oxygen rebreathers that are popular around the world. Included among these are the Spirotechnique Oxy-NG made in France, the Cobra made by Carlton Industries of the U.S., the S-10 developed by Fullerton Sherwood of Canada, and the Dräger

The Dräger LAR V is a fully closed circuit oxygen rebreather that is widely used by the military and government agencies around the world.

LAR V system which is used by the U.S. Navy. All of these systems are almost useless for recreational diving, and are not generally available on the sport diving market.

When people speak of closed circuit mixed gas rebreathers today they are usually referring to an electronically controlled system that mixes oxygen with an inert gas, either helium or nitrogen. These systems have a tremendous depth capability and extended bottom times that are extremely attractive to the technical diver and others who need this type of capability.

All of the closed circuit mixed gas rebreathers on the market today incorporate some electronics in them and for this reason, all require the use of batteries and oxygen sensors. Typically, these rebreathers have redundant sensors so that if one fails, you still will get a reading on your oxygen level. With these systems you must figure on the use of batteries and sensors as part of your operational costs, along with your gas supply and CO_2 absorbent.

Closed circuit mixed gas rebreathers tend to be as heavy or heavier than open circuit scuba systems. Yet, if you tried to carry as many scuba cylinders as would equal the gas duration of a closed circuit rebreather, you would be carrying hundreds of pounds of equipment.

For many years closed circuit rebreathers were not available to the civilian diver, but in the mid-nineties several different models of closed circuit systems were made available to the technical diving market. Some of the closed circuit systems that have become accessible include the Bio-Marine BMR500, the Undersea Technologies UT240, the Prism Topaz from Steam Machines, and the Cis-Lunar. Each of these rebreathers is quite different from the others although all are designed to give extended bottom times at depths far in excess of the 130 foot limit commonly considered as the limit for organized recreational diving.

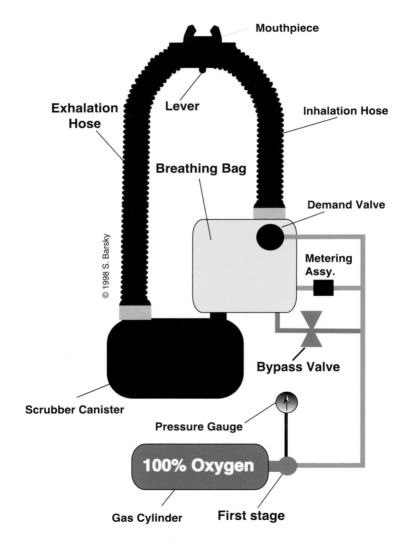

Oxygen rebreathers are the simplest type of rebreather system. This schematic shows the layout of a "typical" oxygen system.

Bio-Marine's system is one of the most commonly used fully closed circuit mixed gas rebreathers.

SEMI-CLOSED CIRCUIT REBREATHERS USING PRE-MIXED GAS

The first modern rebreathers sold for recreational diving were semi-closed circuit rebreathers. These systems use pre-mixed nitrox as the breathing gas; there is no on-board mixing and the systems are strictly mechanically controlled.

As its name implies, a semi-closed circuit rebreather does not recirculate all of the breathing gas from the gas cylinders. These systems introduce a metered, continuous flow of breathing gas into the breathing loop, and exhaust a small, but constant amount of gas with each breath you take.

Semi-closed circuit rebreathers that use pre-mixed gas have a limited depth capability and are generally not designed to be used at depths below 130 feet. In fact, their optimal range is normally from the surface down to about 75 feet. Beyond that depth, the limitations of nitrox come into play and reduce the efficiency of these systems.

The big disadvantage to using a semi-closed circuit rebreather is that you must decide what your maximum diving depth will be at the time you get your cylinder filled. Unless you are on a dive boat with the capability to fill nitrox cylinders, or you have taken several cylinders with you, there is no way to change your gas mixture once you are at the dive site. To some divers this may be a major disadvantage while to others this may pose little or no inconvenience.

Semi-closed circuit rebreathers allow you to use nitrox much more efficiently than open circuit gear, but not as efficiently as a fully closed circuit system. While these systems do not require batteries to operate, they may use batteries to power an onboard oxygen monitoring system. Although the electronics used in these systems will allow you to monitor the oxygen level in the rebreather, they are not designed to make any adjustments to it.

Another important issue to consider when using these systems is that the partial pressure of oxygen (ppO2) in the breathing system will vary according to your exercise level during the dive. Without an accurate oxygen monitoring system, your decompression calculations could be seriously affected by these variations. This topic will be covered in greater detail in Chapter 5 on semi-closed circuit rebreathers.

Semi-closed circuit systems were introduced into the sport diving market in the mid–nineties. These systems are well suited for the recreational diving market.

SEMI-CLOSED CIRCUIT REBREATHERS, SELF-MIXING SYSTEMS

Semi-closed circuit self-mixing systems are more sophisticated than systems that use pre-mixed gas. These systems can be either mechanical or electronic.

The advantage to using a semi-closed circuit self-mixing system is that in areas where pre-mixed nitrox is not available, the system will do the mixing for you. The disadvantage of

Dräger's Dolphin (originally sold as the Atlantis I) was the first commercially successful semi-closed circuit rebreather that was available internationally for recreational diving.

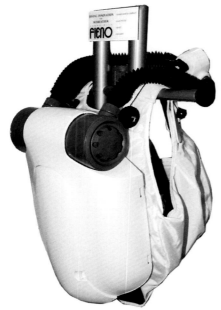

The Fieno from Grand Bleu was available in the Japanese market for several years. It was a compact, semi-closed circuit rebreather.

this type of system is that since it is semi-closed it does not have the efficiency of a fully closed circuit system.

The Prism by Steam Machines is a good example of a rebreather that works in the semi-closed mode. It can be used as either a semi-closed or fully closed circuit system. This is a very advanced capability rebreather with an on-board computer.

The Prism rebreather, developed by Peter Readey, can be used in either the semi-closed circuit mode or the fully closed circuit mode. It is a self-mixing system.

Peter Readey developed the Prism closed circuit rebreather.

IN THE BEGINNING, THERE WERE REBREATHERS...

Long before Jacques Cousteau and Emil Gagnan developed the modern compressed air scuba gear that made recreational diving possible, people were diving with rebreathers. In fact, rebreathers were the first life support gear used for self-contained recreational diving.

At the heart of the rebreather is the concept of the removal of carbon dioxide from a closed breathing system. Before anyone could build a rebreather, this problem had to be solved.

As early as 1777 a Swedish scientist named Scheele discovered that bees could be kept alive in a sealed glass jar by absorbing the carbon dioxide they produced with a solution of lime water. By 1847, another team of French scientists, Regnault and Reiset found that they could keep dogs alive in a sealed chamber by supplying oxygen and removing carbon dioxide with lime. These discoveries were essential to pave the way for the development of the rebreather.

The earliest rebreather on record was the Fleuss Mask, developed in England in the 1880s. Henry Fleuss was a self-taught engineer who became intrigued with the problems of diving when he watched a helmet diver working in the harbor in Ceylon. He believed that there had to be a way to make the diver independent of the air hose and the pump. After reading books on physiology and chemistry, he reasoned that if the diver could carry a supply of oxygen and an alkali to remove carbon dioxide, he could eliminate the air supply from topside.

Henry Fleuss was an amazing man who developed all of the resources for his first rebreather himself, right down to inventing a method to produce and compress his own oxygen. He tested his system in the diving tank at the Royal Polytechnic School in London, under the supervision of a physiologist. Fleuss made a number of dives with the system

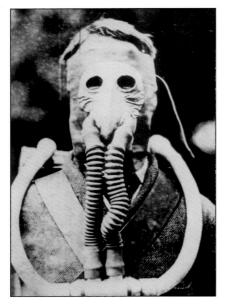

and believed that "too little oxygen is indicated by an uneasy breathing and too much by a feeling of pressure on the ear-drums." Fortunately, we have better information today!

The Fleuss mask was the first known rebreather system to be used underwater.
(Photo courtesy of Siebe-Gorman Co. © Siebe-Gorman. All rights reserved.)

Although Fleuss' rebreather worked, there was more interest in a system for rescuing workers trapped in flooded coal mines. In his earliest design, the breathing bag and the scrubber canister were originally mounted on the diver's back, but there was no protective shroud to house the system.

Fleuss eventually joined forces with the British firm of Siebe-Gorman and continued with the development of rebreathers through them. In 1904 Siebe-Gorman patented a material called "Oxylighte", a chemical compound designed to be used in a rebreather to remove carbon dioxide. Siebe-Gorman remained extremely active in rebreather development through World War II, manufacturing both rebreathers for combat divers as well as submarine escape apparatus, based upon the same technology.

In 1911, Dr. Bernhard Dräger began developing rebreathers in Germany and the Dräger company built a diving simulator for testing rebreathers under controlled conditions the same year. Company records show that on July 17, 1914 their technicians tested a rebreather that allowed a diver to reach a depth of approximately 240 feet for 40 minutes.

Dr. Bernhard Dräger (wearing the hat) started working on rebreathers in 1911.   (*Courtesy Dräger Diving*)

Dräger built its first diving test tank in 1911.

(*Courtesy Dräger Diving*)

By 1926 Dräger had developed a closed circuit oxygen rebreather that they were actively marketing for search and rescue work. An illustration from an early company promotional piece shows a diver wearing street clothes, goggles, and the rebreather climbing over underwater rocks to reach a drowning victim lying on the bottom of a lake.

The first recreational use of rebreathers took place in 1942. Hans Hass, an Austrian marine biologist, was already free diving and using home-made diving helmets to make underwater films in 1941 when he met Hermann Stelzner of Dräger in the spring of that year.

Hass and Stelzner modified a Dräger rebreather, altering the breathing bag and oxygen supply valve. The equipment was used to make Hass' 1942 underwater film, *Man Amongst Sharks*. From that time forward, Hass and his wife, Lotte, used the rebreather almost exclusively in their dives around the world. Together, they produced 26 books and more than 100 films and television shows on diving. Hass also developed the first housing for the Rolleimarin camera, one of the earliest professional housings ever developed for underwater use.

Hans and Lotte Hass became internationally famous for their films and books starting in 1942. They did most of their diving using Dräger rebreathers.

American firms like Desco (Diving Equipment Supply Company) and MSA (Mine Safety Apparatus) built rebreathers that were primarily sold to the military, but also made their way into civilian applications. Colonel John D. Craig, author of the famous diving book, *Danger is My Business*, used a Desco rebreather.

Col. John D. Craig, author of the book, "Danger is My Business", used this closed circuit oxygen system to shoot underwater photos for his books and other projects.

(*Equipment from the collection of Nick Icorn.*)

Mine Safety Apparatus (MSA) designed rebreathers for the military.
(*Equipment from the collection of Nick Icorn.*)

By the late 1950s, open circuit scuba gear had almost completely replaced rebreathers for recreational diving. However, military divers and diving scientists were still using rebreathers, and the concept of a compact, deep diving system never went away. A few companies and individuals scattered around the world were still working quietly on improving rebreather technology.

In 1968, Walter Starck and John Kanwisher developed the Electrolung, one of the first electronic fully closed circuit rebreathers designed for deep mixed-gas diving. It provided up to six hours of dive time using less than ten cubic feet of breathing gas. During the same period, Westinghouse developed an extremely compact pure oxygen rebreather, known as the "Mini-Lung" for espionage purposes.

Westinghouse's Mini-Lung was developed for espionage purposes during the late sixties. It was a fully closed circuit oxygen system.
(Equipment from the collection of Nick Icorn.)

By 1969 the Electrolung was commercially available at a retail price of $2000.00. Beckman Instruments bought the rights to the product and began to market the system aggressively. After three fatalities with the system in 1970, however, Beckman decided that the profits did not justify the liability exposure and discontinued sales of the system. This occurred despite the fact that in at least two of the accidents the evidence pointed overwhelmingly towards diver error.

The Electrolung was the first modern commercially available electronic closed circuit mixed gas rebreather. Bob Stinton of Diving Unlimited International (left) is seen here wearing an Electrolung while Jay Jeffries wears a Bio-Marine 155 system.

The U.S. Navy has been using Bio-Marine's rebreathers for many years and these systems have also been used by underwater photographers like Howard Hall, Marty Snyderman, and John McKenny, son of the late Jack McKenny. The military version of this system is known as the MK16, while the civilian version that has been used by professional photographers is the Bio-Marine 155. The U.S. Navy's MK15 and MK16, manufactured by Carlton Industries, evolved from the original Bio-Marine technology. The Bio-Marine BMR500 is the technical diver's version of this system.

Three views of the Navy MK11 diving system. This was an umbilical fed semi-closed circuit system.

Designed by Bev Morgan, this full face mask could be used in either the open circuit or the semi-closed circuit mode.

The Navy has also used umbilical fed semi-closed circuit systems for many years. The Navy MK11 Mod 0 system became operational in 1974 and included a semi-closed circuit rebreather, a full face mask, and a hot water suit. Bev Morgan of Diving Systems International, designed the full face mask that went with this system. The rebreather was more commonly referred to as the "abalone rig" because of its profile. This system had the capability to support a diver to 1000 FSW in 28 degree F water for up to four hours.

Rebreathers have been built in almost every country and their designs have been extremely varied. Yet, whether they have been built in Russia, France, Germany, England, or the U.S., their operations have always been fundamentally the same. Developing unique high performance rebreathers has been the goal of every designer.

While it wasn't sent from Russia with love, this Russian rebreather made its way to the western world at the end of the cold war. It used two scrubber canisters. (Equipment from the collection of Nick Icorn.)

A variety of rebreathers from little known manufacturers have appeared on the market for a short time and then completely disappeared. One of the smallest and most interesting of these systems was the EOBA, which stood for enriched oxygen breathing apparatus and was developed in Japan.

The EOBA was shown at the Diving Equipment Manufacturer's Association (DEMA) show in the early nineties. It was designed to be used at a maximum depth of 16 feet for 10 minutes. Obviously, this was an extremely limited system that had little market appeal.

By the mid-nineties, new rebreathers were appearing on the market on a regular basis. Although Dräger was the only

The Oxy-NG is a French oxygen rebreather designed by Spirotechnique, one of the sister companies of the Aqualung® Group, which includes U.S. Divers, Co., Inc.

full line manufacturer to sell rebreathers in 1997, we expect the majority of manufacturers to offer their own systems in the next few years.

You might wonder why the rebreather is suddenly popular again. There are two reasons why this has happened. First, nitrox has become commonly available in dive shops around the world. This made the semi-closed circuit rebreather accessible to the average recreational diver. The second issue was the development of the modern microprocessor, which provided improved electronics for oxygen monitoring and "on-the-fly" decompression calculations with changing oxygen partial pressures. This made the fully closed circuit rebreather more reliable and brought costs down to a more reasonable level.

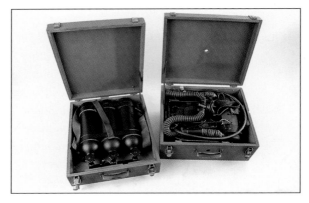

The Fenzy P-68 was another French system designed for mixed-gas with a 600 foot depth capability. The cylinders were designed to be worn on the chest and the breathing bag went on the diver's back.

(Equipment from the collection of Nick Icorn.)

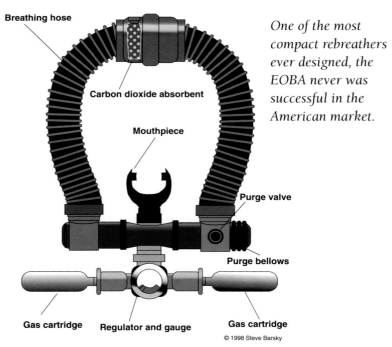

One of the most compact rebreathers ever designed, the EOBA never was successful in the American market.

Breathing hose

Carbon dioxide absorbent

Mouthpiece

Purge valve

Purge bellows

Gas cartridge   Regulator and gauge   Gas cartridge

© 1998 Steve Barsky

THE FUTURE OF REBREATHERS

In the future, we expect to see smaller and more compact rebreathers, although it appears there will always be certain practical limitations to the size and weight of these systems. For example, the breathing bags (also known as the counter lungs) must hold a sufficient volume of breathing gas so the diver can breathe comfortably. The size of the bags has a direct impact on your buoyancy, and you must carry appropriate weight to offset them. Similarly, the breathing hoses must be of a sufficient diameter to allow easy breathing. The scrubber must hold enough carbon dioxide absorbent to see you through a dive with some reserve capacity as well.

By the time you add in a bail-out system and a buoyancy compensator, you can see that there is a practical limit to how small a rebreather can be and still work. Future advancements in rebreathers will almost certainly be primarily in the electronics for managing oxygen levels, decompression, and alarms. We can expect advances in CO_2 scrubbing materials, such as water tolerant granular or sieve type systems. Another possibility is the use of liquid chemical catalysts for carbon dioxide removal or reusable absorbents. All of these will add to the safety and efficiency of closed circuit systems.

Better monitoring systems and computers that automatically monitor your oxygen level will become commonly available. Ideally, future rebreathers will feature fast response oxygen sensors which will allow significantly lower gas injection rates because the diver will be able to monitor the exact percentage of oxygen in the system.

Open circuit scuba, because of its greater simplicity and lower cost, will probably never be completely replaced by rebreathers. However, rebreathers will become more common and their use will increase over time.

CHAPTER 2

APPLICATIONS FOR REBREATHERS

Like most things in life, no matter what type of diving equipment you use, it will have advantages and disadvantages when compared to other similar gear. For example, a wetsuit is cheaper to purchase than a dry suit, but a dry suit will generally keep you warmer. The wetsuit may be easier to maintain, but a quality dry suit will have a longer useful service life. There are similar advantages and disadvantages to rebreathers.

Picking the right diving gear for a particular application is like picking the right tool to do a home improvement project. Do you need a plastic hammer or a four pound steel sledge?

If you are going to dive in six feet of water on a tropical reef, snorkeling equipment may be all that you need. To make a single dive off the beach in a geothermal lake in Utah at 30 feet, open circuit scuba may be the best choice. To dive to 70 feet on a wreck off the coast of southern California, a semi-closed circuit rebreather would be a good choice.

Diving scientists working to study pollution in a harbor off Greece may find that surface supplied diving gear with hard wire communications is the optimal gear for their work. Cave divers exploring a deep, extended cave system in Mexico would probably be best served by diving with a fully closed circuit rebreather.

By selecting the right gear for your specific needs you will enhance your safety and efficiency in the water. Being overequipped for a dive is expensive and wasteful of money and resources, while being underequipped could be dangerous or even fatal.

Picking the right diving gear for a particular dive is crucial to your success. In many cases, open circuit gear may be more economical and practical than using a rebreather.

To make the right decision about which particular piece of dive gear is correct for a particular application, you need to understand its advantages and disadvantages. In addition you must consider the characteristics of the particular rebreather you intend to use before you can decide whether it suits your purpose.

ADVANTAGES OF REBREATHERS

The main advantages to using a rebreather include the following:

- Rebreathers provide more efficient use of breathing gas.
- Rebreathers supply warm, moist breathing gas.
- Semi-closed circuit rebreathers offer very quiet operation, while fully closed circuit rebreathers offer nearly silent operation.
- Rebreathers have significant advantages in supplying either the optimum, or near optimum, oxygen partial pressure for any given depth.

   Although these characteristics of rebreathers may seem simple, understanding them fully will give you a better insight to how rebreathers can best be used.

GAS EFFICIENCY

   The number one advantage of a rebreather over conventional open circuit scuba equipment is its great efficiency in its use of breathing gas. Rebreathers are much more economical to use when you are using nitrox and especially so if you are using helium or trimix.

   While semi-closed circuit rigs can be as much as three times more efficient in their gas utilization than open circuit scuba, fully closed circuit rigs can be as much as ten times more efficient. This efficiency can be advantageous in several ways, whether you want to make one long uninterrupted dive or multiple dives on the same gas cylinder. Either way, the rebreather will give you more bottom time than you can get on an open circuit system.

   Carrying one or two small rebreather cylinders to and from a dive shop to have them filled is not nearly as unpleasant as carrying multiple 80 cubic foot cylinders from your car to the store. The small size and weight of rebreather cylinders is dramatically different from the comparable weight and bulk of open circuit scuba.

Taking your rebreather cylinders to be filled is a lot less work than lugging open circuit scuba cylinders to and from the dive shop.

WARM, MOIST BREATHING GAS

Another major advantage to using a rebreather is the fact that you are breathing warm, moist gas rather than the cold, dehumidified gas provided by open circuit apparatus. With open circuit scuba, the gas in the cylinder, whether it is air, nitrox, or trimix, has been dehumidified prior to filling the cylinder. When this gas is inhaled, it picks up moisture from the wet tissues of your lungs. When you exhale, this moisture is lost which leads to dehydration of your body. This can make you more susceptible to decompression sickness.

With open circuit scuba, as you breathe, the air from your high pressure cylinder expands as it is reduced from cylinder pressure to the surrounding (ambient) pressure, causing it to cool down. When this cold gas is inhaled, it is warmed to body temperature. When you exhale, this heat is lost which leads to fatigue, as well as possible hypothermia and increased susceptibility to decompression sickness.

By comparison, with each breath that you take with a rebreather you are breathing gas that has been heated by both your body and the chemical reaction in the scrubber. In addition, the chemical reaction in the scrubber also liberates moisture, which helps to prevent dehydration.

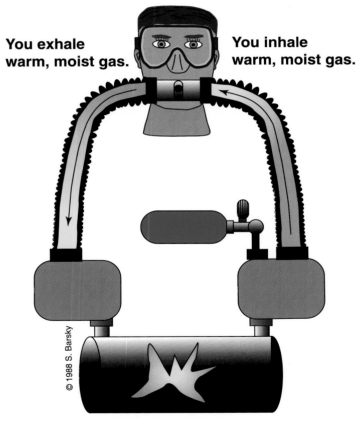

Heat and moisture are generated in the scrubber.

Rebreathers supply warm, moist breathing gas.

SILENT, OR NEAR SILENT OPERATION

Semi-closed circuit rebreathers offer nearly silent operation, while fully closed circuit rebreathers provide virtually silent operation. For the underwater photographer, this can be a major advantage when dealing with certain types of animals, such as the schooling hammerhead sharks found in Mexico's Sea of Cortez.

Since semi-closed circuit rebreathers do give off small bubbles on a regular basis, these systems do not have the totally "silent" operation that is a characteristic of fully closed circuit units. However, when the original Dräger Atlantis systems were shipped they were manufactured with a bubble diffuser that would break up the exhaust into a fine mist of tiny bubbles, similar to the size of those found in a bottle of soda. Government officials decided that there was too much potential for these systems to be used for clandestine military operations and manufacture of the diffuser was discontinued.

Fully closed circuit systems give off no exhaust bubbles except during ascent, and these systems are the preferred systems for professional underwater filmmakers. Yet few filmmakers report that using the rebreather gives them a tremendous competitive edge when it comes to making contact with marine life. Many rebreather divers have found that to most underwater creatures, a human being is still a large, intimidating animal that appears threatening to many smaller reef inhabitants.

While there may be few or no bubbles with some rebreathers, there may be other noises created by the system including those created by solenoid addition valves, bypass valves, audio alarms, and check valves. Don't count on your rebreather to make you "invisible" underwater.

A rebreather may allow you to get closer to animals that otherwise might be difficult to approach due to the absence of exhaust bubbles.

OPTIMUM, OR NEAR OPTIMUM OXYGEN PARTIAL PRESSURE

When you dive with open circuit scuba on air, the percentage of oxygen is fixed at 20.9%. However, the partial pressure varies with the depth. The deeper you dive, the greater the partial pressure of each gas in the air mixture.

At extreme depths the partial pressure of oxygen in air will be too high. At shallower depths, the partial pressure of the oxygen in air is not at the optimal level for decompression.

When you dive with nitrox on open circuit, you again have a fixed percentage of oxygen and its partial pressure varies with the depth. Open circuit nitrox is very restrictive when it comes to your maximum allowable depth for a given mixture. However, bottom times with nitrox are greatly extended compared to what they are when you breathe air.

Similarly, diving with nitrox in a semi-closed circuit rebreather also limits your maximum depth for a given mixture. However, if you choose, you have the ability to take advantage of the extended bottom times provided by nitrox because of the efficiency of the rebreather. Keep in mind, however, that when you use nitrox to extend your bottom time you eliminate any safety factor that you might gain from using it, in regards to your decompression obligation.

Fully closed circuit electronic rebreathers provide the greatest advantage when it comes to maintaining an optimal partial pressure of oxygen. This is what gives the fully closed circuit electronic rebreather its superiority for deep diving and decompression diving.

On a deep dive, with a properly functioning self-mixing electronic unit, you will always receive the exact partial pressure of oxygen that you need (provided the system is working properly!). During decompression, you can elevate the percentage of oxygen all the way to close to 100% for your shallower decompression stops. This can help reduce the risk of decompression sickness.

Fully closed circuit rebreathers offer tremendous advantages for deep or decompression diving.

DISADVANTAGES OF REBREATHERS

Rebreathers have some definite disadvantages over traditional open circuit scuba that make them unattractive for some applications. The disadvantages of rebreathers include the following:

- Rebreathers are more expensive to purchase than open circuit scuba.
- Rebreathers can be as heavy, or heavier than open circuit scuba
- Operating costs with rebreathers are more expensive than with open circuit air diving gear.
- Rebreathers require more pre-dive preparation time than open circuit scuba.
- Post-dive maintenance with a rebreather requires more time than with open circuit scuba gear.
- Rebreathers are more complex to use than open circuit scuba gear.
- Medical grade oxygen, pure diluent (inert gas), and carbon dioxide absorbent may not be readily available in certain diving locations.

REBREATHERS ARE EXPENSIVE

It is generally recognized that rebreathers are more expensive to purchase than open circuit equipment, but of course, they give you more capability. The big question that you must consider is whether or not you can take full advantage of the capabilities of the rebreather you plan to buy.

For example, if you dive in cold water, unless you use a dry suit and a dive computer, it is unlikely that you will be able to make use of the extended bottom time that a rebreather offers. Even if you dive in warm water, you will probably need some thermal protection during extended dives.

It's important to keep in mind that there may also be other costs associated with your rebreather purchase such as bail-out systems, special lubricants, oxygen analyzers, additional weights, disinfectants, and other minor maintenance items.

If you are a sport diver, how do you justify the cost of a semi-closed circuit system? Probably the best application for a semi-closed circuit rebreather is for people who regularly dive from a small boat in a remote location where no air compressor is available. The capabilities of even a simple semi-closed circuit system will allow you to dive for an entire weekend, at moderate depths, on two small (30 cu. ft.) cylinders of gas per diver, rather than loading your boat with six, 80 cubic foot cylinders per person.

If you own a small boat, a rebreather can save you a considerable amount of deck space and weight over the course of a weekend of diving.

For technical divers who regularly dive in overhead environments, such as caves or wrecks; or engage in deep, decompression diving; the fully closed circuit electronic rebreather is the ideal piece of equipment. It makes far more sense to dive with a rebreather than to carry multiple gas cylinders with you during a long, tiring dive.

On extended dives over 200 feet it is impossible to carry as many scuba cylinders as would be required to equal the bottom time and decompression gas provided by a rebreather like Bio-Marine's, the Prism Topaz, or the Cis-Lunar system. Gas costs for helium are also much less expensive using a rebreather. In addition, it is much safer not to have to remove your mouthpiece to make a gas change as you would with open circuit scuba.

REBREATHERS ARE NOT LIGHT WEIGHT

A fully rigged rebreather system is in most cases, as heavy, or heavier than a fully rigged 80 cubic foot scuba cylinder with buoyancy compensator and regulator. For example, the Dräger Atlantis I system, when fully rigged with carbon dioxide absorbent, bail-out bottle and regulator, weighs in at over 45 pounds. Lighter systems are certainly possible, as demonstrated by the Japanese Fieno (no longer in production). Bio-Marine's BMR500 also weighs in at 45 pounds, minus any counterweights.

Again while the weight of the fully rigged system is at least equal to most scuba rigs, the advantage of the rebreather is in the elimination of the weight and bulk of multiple cylinders.

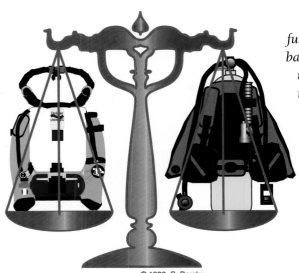

When they are fully rigged with bail-out systems, rebreathers are not any lighter than a fully rigged open circuit scuba system.

© 1998. S. Barsky

COST TO OPERATE

Using a rebreather, your dive costs for nitrox, heliox, or trimix gases are far less than what they are using open circuit equipment. However, when you factor in the cost of batteries and carbon dioxide absorbent the cost to operate may still be more expensive than on open circuit depending on your breathing medium. Of course, what doesn't factor into the equation is the convenience of using the rebreather compared to the weight and bulk of multiple gas cylinders.

For a semi-closed circuit rebreather, like the Dräger Atlantis system, we have calculated costs of approximately $5.76 for 40 minutes of dive time in 1997 using nitrox 40/60. In most situations, it is still more expensive to dive with a rebreather than open circuit air, but less expensive than diving with nitrox on open circuit, on a per dive basis.

For systems like Bio-Marine's, the operating costs for the rebreather run about $8.00 per hour. This figure includes both carbon dioxide absorbent and batteries, which run $20.00 per set and last for 14 hours. Efficient gas utilization is the key to the economics of diving with a rebreather.

Maintenance costs are part of your operational costs, and the maintenance of a rebreather will definitely be more expensive than that of conventional scuba equipment. Replacement of breathing hoses and bags is expensive as well as other components. Your bail-out regulator and cylinder will also need annual service. Your oxygen analyzer will need batteries and fuel cells. As a starting point, figure that your annual system maintenance will probably be about five to eight times what you will spend to maintain open circuit gear!

MORE PREPARATION TO DIVE

Setting up a semi-closed circuit mechanical rebreather takes about 15 minutes for an experienced diver. This includes the time it takes to fill the scrubber canister, install the cylinder, rig the bailout, assemble the breathing bags, install the hoses, and test all the connections. Although this isn't a significant amount of time, it's definitely longer than the two minutes it might take to set up an open circuit system.

Setting up an electronic self-mixing rebreather may take 30-45 minutes or longer. With a fully closed circuit electronic system you have two gas cylinders instead of one and you are also dealing with a battery and electronic system. This takes additional time beyond what it takes to set up a simpler semi-closed circuit mechanical system.

There are no short cuts that can be taken in setting up a rebreather system properly. Become careless with any of the required steps or safety checks and you may end up a diving fatality.

Setting up a rebreather for diving takes more time than setting up open circuit scuba.

MORE POST-DIVE MAINTENANCE

Post dive maintenance with a rebreather is more time consuming than it is with open circuit scuba. In addition, the maintenance of your rebreather must be done promptly and with more care than most people give to their open circuit gear.

With a rebreather, there are numerous components that must be dealt with, properly cleaned and in some cases, properly dried. This may require additional accessories beyond what is required to maintain ordinary scuba.

Many rebreather divers feel it is essential to disinfect their breathing system to avoid the growth of fungus and bacteria. This becomes more important if you are diving in a hot, humid climate; if there isn't sufficient time between dives for all of the system components to dry completely; and/or if multiple divers are using the same rebreather. In situations where the above conditions are not a concern, air drying the equipment is usually sufficient to prevent problems.

In addition to disinfecting your rebreather, you may also want to hasten drying time by building a drying cabinet that circulates cool, dry air in and around your system's components. Whatever method you choose, it is essential to ensure that your rebreather is completely dry during any extended storage period.

Maintaining a rebreather is more complex than maintaining open circuit scuba.

MORE COMPLEXITY

Aside from the fact that rebreathers require more time to set up and maintain, diving with a rebreather is more complicated than diving with open circuit gear. There are more components that can fail and there are more physiological risks than there are when diving with compressed air scuba.

Diving with a rebreather requires a high level of knowledge of the medical/physiological aspects of diving. You must also be extremely disciplined in regards to your dive planning and decompression, as well as your back-up options in the event that something goes wrong.

With a fully closed circuit rebreather you can incur an outrageous decompression obligation if you are not conservative. Combine an extreme decompression obligation with a rebreather failure and inadequate back-up supply and you have a recipe for disaster.

The mechanical risks that you must consider when you dive with a rebreather include the following:

- Carbon dioxide absorbent failure
- Scrubber leakage
- Injector blockage
- Inhalation/exhalation bag failure
- Breathing hose failure
- Regulator failure
- Electronic failure (if your system includes such components)

Any one of these failures is sufficient to cause a serious or fatal accident. Multiple failures during a single dive would expose you to an extremely high level of risk.

Some of the physiological risks that occur with rebreathers can never occur if you dive with open circuit scuba. These risks include hypoxia, carbon dioxide toxicity, and exposure to caustic chemicals. Oxygen toxicity can become a risk at a much shallower depth than it would if you dive only with compressed air.

When you dive with a rebreather you must monitor more signals from the system than you do when you dive with ordinary scuba. For example, if your system includes an oxygen

Don't attempt complex tasks, such as underwater photography, during a dive until you are completely comfortable diving with your rebreather.

monitor you must be aware of the level of oxygen in your system at all times. Similarly, you must be monitoring the sounds of the system bypass regulator, be alert for the sounds of water in your scrubber canister, and be in tune with the movement of the breathing bags in your system.

All of these different functions that you must monitor and control as you dive contribute to what is known as your "task loading". The greater number of tasks that you must perform, the more complex your dive becomes, and the higher your potential is for accidents. This is one of the reasons why your initial dives with a rebreather should be focused strictly on training. Other activities, such as underwater photography, that interfere with your attention, should not be attempted until you are comfortable with your rebreather.

AVAILABILITY OF BREATHING GAS AND ABSORBENT MATERIAL

Filling a scuba tank with compressed air is a simple task that requires no special skill or equipment. However, filling a gas cylinder with nitrox is a different matter, and requires special equipment, knowledge, and training. For these reasons, nitrox is not available in all dive stores and probably never will be.

Even fewer dive stores are prepared to sell pure helium, pure oxygen, or other exotic gases. In many areas you may be forced to go to one location to fill your scuba bail-out and another location to get the gas you need if you are diving with an electronically controlled self-mixing rebreather. For example, you may need to go to an industrial gas supplier to purchase pure helium or heliox.

In remote locations, although breathing gas may be available, carbon dioxide absorbent will usually be non-existent unless you bring it with you. This material is bulky and heavy and will easily put you over the limit on your baggage allowance if you are traveling by air.

You may need to visit an industrial gas supplier to purchase pure helium for rebreather diving.

APPLICATIONS FOR REBREATHERS

For recreational diving, the biggest advantage to using a rebreather is in eliminating the need to carry multiple scuba tanks aboard a small boat. With a semi-closed circuit system and a 60% oxygen mixture you can carry enough breathing gas for six shallow dives of 40 minutes duration in two 30 cubic foot breathing cylinders. For most people this would represent an entire weekend of diving.

Aside from the obvious applications for rebreathers that have already been mentioned, such as photography and technical diving, there are many other places where a rebreather can be extremely advantageous. These activities include scientific diving and search and rescue diving.

Professional underwater photographers like Howard Hall use rebreathers to provide themselves with extended bottom times. This Imax camera has been used by Hall in several of his outstanding films. (© *Mark Conlin/Imax. All rights reserved.*)

Scientific divers find that rebreathers are advantageous for the same reasons that underwater photographers and technical divers like rebreathers. In particular, scientific divers appreciate the ability to dive deeper with greater safety and to silently approach wary animals. Marine biologist Richard Pyle has discovered numerous new species of fish throughout the South Pacific diving with a rebreather from Cis-Lunar.

The California Department of Fish and Game and the U.S. Fish and Wildlife Service have both used Dräger LAR V rebreathers to capture and tag sea otters. The rebreathers provided an ideal tool for this work in that it allows the biologists to approach these intelligent animals, undetected, from below, to capture them with a special trap. The technique did not work with open circuit scuba because the bubbles spooked the otters and alerted them to the diver's presence.

Public safety divers will undoubtedly find new applications for rebreathers that may include diving in polluted waters and tactical diving in hostage rescue situations or other police action. However, given the expense of most rebreathers, the majority of law enforcement agencies will probably find that they must have a demonstrated need before their department will be willing to spring for this type of gear.

Christine Pattison, a biologist with the California Dept. of Fish and Game, prepares to dive with a Dräger LAR V, as part of the sea otter recovery program dive team.

CHAPTER 3

COMMON ELEMENTS OF REBREATHER DESIGN

All rebreathers have certain common elements, no matter whether they are semi-closed circuit mechanical systems or fully closed circuit computerized units. Every rebreather must include a breathing gas supply, a scrubber canister, breathing bags, pressure reducing regulators, pressure gauges, and breathing hoses. Less expensive rebreathers are generally built with as many "off-the-shelf" components as possible, while more expensive systems will use parts that have been specifically designed for that particular system.

Rebreather designs vary widely as various inventors have developed different ways to solve the same problems. Some solutions have worked better than others, but there is very little to regulate how a particular rebreather addresses a particular performance aspect.

In the United States, the U.S. Navy Experimental Diving Unit (NEDU) in Panama City, Florida, tests rebreathers designed for military use. They also test certain civilian diving equipment if it shows promise for possible military applications. Navy tests typically include both human factors evaluations as well as physiological performance tests.

Human factors testing evaluates the physical design of the equipment from the perspective of ease of use by the diver. This might include how easy it is to set the unit up and per-

The Navy Experimental Diving Unit (NEDU) tests rebreathers to determine whether they meet the needs of military divers.

form maintenance, the placement of controls, and subjective measures of diver comfort. Other measures that come under the heading of human factors (ergonomics) might include determinations of the effect of the system on the diver's center of buoyancy, readability of any integrated dive computers or oxygen sensors, and evaluation of the user manual.

Navy physiological evaluations for rebreathers will typically include tests for work of breathing, canister breakthrough time, and breathing bag oxygen levels. Minimum standards have been established by the Navy for breathing systems to be acceptable for their divers' needs. However, just because a system has been approved for Navy use does not mean that it is acceptable for recreational diving applications.

In Europe, diving equipment is tested by a variety of independent testing organizations, and the current requirement for diving equipment to be sold in Europe is the "CE" mark. The CE mark means that the product conforms with all European Community laws and standards. The quality standard that companies must now meet is ISO 9000 and has been adopted worldwide.

Rebreathers are tested in both manned and unmanned tests at the chamber at NEDU.

Standards for CE testing of rebreathers had not been finalized as of January 1998. It is important to keep in mind , that CE certification does not guarantee that a piece of equipment is totally safe. The main intent of CE testing is to verify the manufacturer's claims regarding the product's performance and operational capabilities.

The information in this chapter has been designed to provide you with some helpful guidelines in evaluating any rebreather you are considering purchasing. Before you purchase a rebreather, be sure to read this chapter and talk to your instructor and other divers about their experiences using specific rebreather models. Don't purchase a rebreather unless you have had the opportunity to try a particular unit and see if it seems like a system you can comfortably use.

FIRST STAGE REGULATOR

All rebreathers require at least one first stage high pressure reduction regulator. Self-mixing rebreathers will have two high pressure regulators, one for pure oxygen and one for the diluent gas, which may be pure gas, but is more commonly either nitrox or heliox.

In most cases, the first stage regulators will be standard off-the-shelf units for which parts will be readily available. Units used for pure oxygen service must be cleaned for this application and the o-rings,lubricants, and seats used in them must be oxygen compatible.

CARBON DIOXIDE (CO2)ABSORBENTS CHEMICAL ABSORBENTS

Although chemical carbon dioxide absorbents are not a permanent physical feature in a rebreather, they are essential to all conventional rebreather designs. Without this consumable item, none of the rebreathers available at the time of this writing would work.

Chemical absorbents are the traditional method of removing carbon dioxide from closed breathing systems. There have been a variety of compounds developed for use in rebreathers, most notably lithium hydroxide and soda lime.

The most commonly used chemical CO_2 absorbent is soda lime, a mixture of caustic soda (NaOH - sodium hydroxide) and lime ($Ca(OH)_2$ - calcium hydroxide). Potassium hydroxide (KOH) is also usually included in the mixture. While lithium hydroxide works better than soda lime at low temperatures, it is a more expensive compound and is more caustic when wet.

The absorbent that is used in rebreathers is used in a similar form in other applications including submarines, anesthesia, and rebreathers used by miners. However, the compounds that have been developed for diving have characteristics that make them especially suitable for this function. For this reason, you should use only absorbent that is designated for use in diving equipment. Products that fall under this category include High Performance Sodasorb® manufactured by W.R. Grace, Divesorb® manufactured by Dräger, Sodalime from

Puritan Bennett, and Sofnolime® manufactured by Molecular Products.

Sodasorb® is manufactured by W.R. Grace.

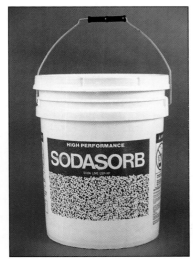

Sodalime, from Puritan Bennett Corp., is another popular absorbent.

Care should be taken when handling chemical CO_2 absorbents since these items are caustic in nature. You should wear gloves, eye protection, and a chemical mask to avoid inhaling chemical dust. Be sure to obtain a copy of the MSDS (Material Safety Data Sheet) for the particular absorbent you are using so that you know the safe handling procedures, as well as first aid measures if the material gets on your skin, in your eyes, your lungs, or is accidentally swallowed.

Absorbent should always be poured into your canister from a height of at least a foot above the canister itself. This will allow absorbent dust to be carried away from the canister by the wind. Dust tends to settle into the bottom of the absorbent container so avoid using the last inch or so of absorbent from the bottom of the drum.

A certain amount of moisture is essential to get the reaction in the scrubber started. The soda lime itself will contain some moisture (about 12%-15%) and your exhaled breath will contain moisture from your lungs. This is normally sufficient to get the reaction going. If the moisture content is too high, however, such as through partial flooding of the rebreather, the reaction will definitely be hampered.

Good canister design allows the exhaled gas to slow down or "dwell", allowing the chemical conversion process to continue at a fairly even rate until the absorbent has converted all the carbon dioxide it can. As a general rule, for every liter of oxygen that is consumed by the body, a liter of carbon dioxide is produced. Eventually, a point is reached where the reaction starts to slow down because the absorbent material has reached the end of its conversion capacity. At this point, CO_2 levels will start to rise very quickly. This is called the "breakthrough point" of the canister. Keep in mind that whenever you are diving in water colder than 40 degrees F the duration of the canister's effectiveness will be significantly reduced.

The chemical reaction that occurs when the absorbent combines with carbon dioxide liberates both heat and moisture. Although attempts have been made to quantify the amount of heat and moisture released as a result of this reaction, it is hard to give exact figures since the amount of each of the by-products created is dependent on a variety of factors. In one experiment, where a canister was submerged in 68° F water, the highest exit gas temperature was 98.6° F! Keep in mind that this temperature would have been recorded at the peak of the reaction, and that prior to, and after the peak, the temperature would not be as great.

In warm tropical waters it is possible that the heat released by the chemical reaction in the scrubber could cause you to become hyperthermic (overheated), especially if you are working hard. This is another good reason to slow down and

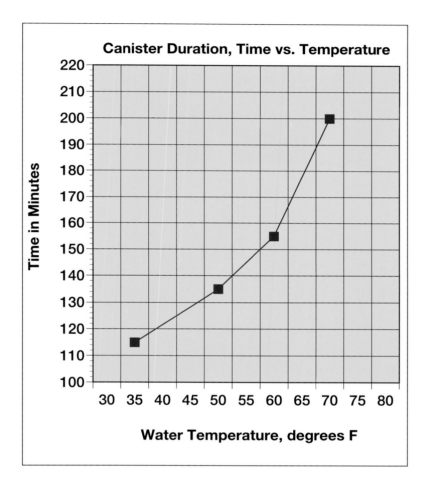

Canister Duration, Time vs. Temperature

The effectiveness of the absorbent is highly dependent on the temperature. This chart shows the approximate times that can be expected from a Dräger LAR V oxygen rebreather canister at various temperatures. As you can see, the colder the water, the less effective the absorbent becomes.

(Source: U.S. Navy Diving Manual, Vol. 2, Mixed Gas Diving, 1991)

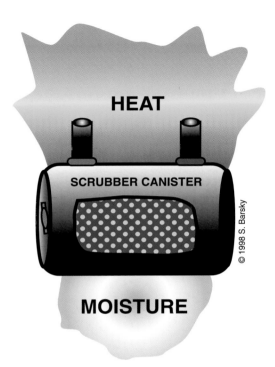

HEAT

SCRUBBER CANISTER

© 1998 S. Barsky

MOISTURE

The byproducts of the absorbent reaction are heat and moisture.

catch your breath if you find yourself breathing heavily underwater. High breathing rates in warm waters will only serve to make the chemical reaction accelerate and worsen the problem if you don't slow down and allow your breathing rate to get back to normal.

Most, but not all, chemical absorbents have a color indicator that signifies when the absorbent is spent. For example, Sodasorb® turns from white to violet once the capacity of the absorbent to neutralize CO_2 has been reached. Dräger's Divesorb® is equipped with no such mechanism.

The color indication must never be used to make judgments regarding the remaining capacity of the absorbent. It is a gross indicator only. For example, the color change of the absorbent is never uniform throughout the canister, but usually most dramatic at the inlet end of the canister.

Absorbents that use color indicators are subject to a phenomenon known as "color reversion", where the color indicator disappears if the absorbent is allowed to sit unused for a few hours. You may hear people mistakenly use the term "regeneration" to describe this event, but this is a misleading term. There is no regeneration or renewed capacity of the absorbent to neutralize additional carbon dioxide once it has been used. Spent soda lime must be discarded.

Check for the color change in your absorbent if a color indicator is present. Some absorbents change from white to violet when used

Soda lime is available in different granular (mesh) sizes. The duration of any canister is directly proportional to the absorbent's reactive surface area. For this reason, it is important to know what mesh size the rebreather uses, and if the rebreather can be used with other mesh sizes. Different mesh size absorbents will provide different dive times.

In most instances, smaller grains of absorbent will allow the canister to work longer, but may make it more difficult to move gas through the rebreather, making it harder to breathe. Smaller mesh size absorbents can cost twice as much as hospital grade absorbents.

Frequently when you empty your canister you will note that the absorbent has "caked" or clumped together. This is undesirable since this clumping increases the breathing resistance of your system and decreases the absorption capacity of the soda lime.

Neither used nor unused soda lime is considered a hazardous waste, but that doesn't mean that this material should be disposed of carelessly. Consult with local authorities regarding the proper method of disposal in your area. In most cases, used soda lime may be discarded with your ordinary household trash.

OTHER METHODS OF REMOVING CARBON DIOXIDE

In the future there will undoubtedly be scrubbers that are based upon electronics rather than chemical reactions. Several rebreather manufacturers are developing products that will work this way. An electronic scrubber would not require chemicals and could conceivably be much smaller and lighter, although it would require batteries.

Another type of carbon dioxide removal system is known as a "molecular sieve". This is a device that will only allow molecules of a certain size to pass through a microscopic screen. The molecular sieve concept has been used in a variety of applications in industry, however it requires a large pressure gradient (pressure difference between two compartments) to operate efficiently.

Other future possible scrubbing devices might include the use of semi-permeable membranes and cryogenics. Semi-permeable membranes are materials that will only allow certain gases to pass through them in one direction. Systems could be designed that would only allow carbon dioxide to pass through them one way.

Cryogenics would take advantage of the use of super coolants. Systems that rely on cryogenics perform based on the fact that different gases freeze at different temperatures, allowing carbon dioxide to be separated from the other gases in the breathing mix.

SCRUBBER CANISTER DESIGN

Scrubber canisters have not changed greatly since the earliest designs were developed. All canisters that use chemical absorbents must perform the following basic functions:

- It must have an inlet opening where the gas that has just been exhaled enters the unit.

- It must have an exhaust opening where the cleansed gas can exit the scrubber.

- It must have a removable lid that allows the canister to be both easily filled prior to a dive and emptied when the absorbent is spent.

- It must have a baffle system to ensure an irregular gas flow, so that the gas is exposed to as much of the absorbent as possible, rather than only contacting the same absorbent over and over again.

- It must be constructed so that absorbent material cannot escape from the canister into the breathing loop.

- It should have different size, shape, or color coded fittings so that it is less likely that you will make a mistake in assembling your rebreather.

- It must have a positive method of sealing so that no water can enter the canister during the dive.

- It must be easily cleaned following each dive.

Although it might seem wise to use the largest scrubber possible, to ensure yourself the maximum dive time available, the larger the scrubber the more bulk and weight you must deal with during a dive. The ideal scrubber is the smallest scrubber that will allow you to complete the longest dive you

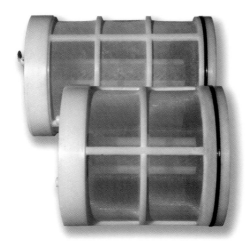

The canisters used in the Prism Topaz rebreather are very small, yet extremely efficient.
(Courtsey of Steam Machines, Inc.)

plan to make. Keep in mind that scrubber performance will vary with your exercise rate, the type of absorbent you use, the water temperature, and the moisture level in the absorbent. Of these factors, the most important are water temperature and exercise rate.

At low water temperatures scrubber performance declines dramatically. For this reason, if you plan to dive under the ice or in areas where the water temperature is below 50 degrees F, you will need to insulate your scrubber. This can usually be accomplished by making a sleeve of wetsuit material to go around the canister. Consult the manufacturer of your rebreather for specific advice in regards to your particular application. Keep in mind that when a manufacturer rates a scrubber for a particular duration that rating will only be under a given set of conditions. If your dives differ from those conditions you cannot expect the same performance from the scrubber.

Most scrubbers resemble large soup cans, although the gas flows through each scrubber design in a different way. There are two main types of chemical absorbent scrubber canisters; they

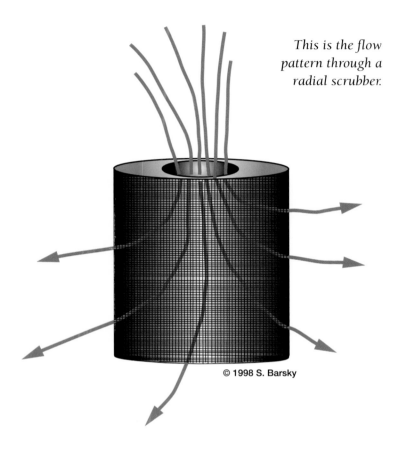

This is the flow pattern through a radial scrubber.

© 1998 S. Barsky

are the radial design and the linear (or axial) design. In a radial scrubber, the gas usually flows up through the center of the scrubber and then out through the sides. In a linear scrubber, the gas flows from one end of the can to the other, in a theoretically "straight" line. Some rebreather designers feel that the radial design is better in reducing overall breathing resistance.

Scrubber canisters with a smooth internal wall suffer from a phenomenon where the gas will tend to flow along this smooth surface as it seeks the path of least resistance through the scrubber. For this reason, companies like Dräger use a removable rubber baffle inside their scrubbers which is

This is the flow pattern through a linear scrubber.

installed as the scrubber is filled. This forces the gas to move through the center of the scrubber where it will be surrounded by absorbent, making the scrubber more efficient.

BREATHING BAG DESIGN

The earliest breathing bags were made from canvas that had been coated with different chemicals to make them waterproof and this was the standard up through World War II. Since that time many new synthetic materials have been used to manufacture breathing bags, with varying degrees of success.

Breathing bags usually have several purposes in most systems, depending upon the design of the rebreather. First, and most importantly, they provide a compliant (flexible) volume roughly equal to the average human lung capacity. Without this volume of gas, a normal inhalation and exhalation cycle would be impossible when using a rebreather. Additionally, the size, shape, and volume of the breathing bags determines the performance capabilities of the rebreather, as well as how the gas from the scrubber mixes with new gas entering the system. The breathing bags can also directly effect the performance of the canister by determining the amount of time the gas will "dwell" in the scrubber canister.

Some rebreathers have both an inhalation bag and an exhalation bag while others may have a single bag. Most dual bag rebreathers are semi-closed circuit systems.

Desirable characteristics for breathing bags include the following:

- The bags must be made from a durable material that is resistant to salt water, sunlight, high and low temperatures, and the chemical absorbent used in the rebreather.

- The bags must be manufactured with a uniform thickness with no thin spots where they are susceptible to wear.

- The bags must hold a sufficient volume of gas to provide comfortable breathing for the largest diver.

- The bags must have a baffle system so that even if water gets inside them, or moisture condenses in them from your exhalations, that water will not enter the scrubber or the breathing hoses.

- The bags should be equipped with shape, size, or color coded fittings to make it less likely that you will make a mistake in assembling your rebreather. These distinctions help eliminate the possibility of improper assembly.

Most breathing bags will have some type of spacer inside them to prevent the bag from collapsing completely when the diver is working hard. The spacer must be soft enough so that it will not damage the bag should it collapse.

Breathing bags may be positioned in one of three locations; on the diver's back, on the diver's chest, or over the

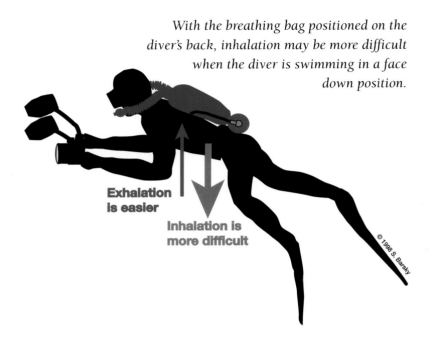

With the breathing bag positioned on the diver's back, inhalation may be more difficult when the diver is swimming in a face down position.

diver's shoulders spanning the upper chest to the upper back. Where the bags are positioned can have a dramatic impact on the breathing characteristics of your rebreather.

When the breathing bags are positioned on your back, inhalation may be slightly more difficult than exhalation if you are swimming in a face down position. This occurs because your lungs are at a greater pressure than the gas in the breathing bags. In essence, you are trying to suck the gas down to your lungs when you inhale. If you turn over on your back when you are wearing a rebreather with back mounted breathing bags, inhalation will suddenly be much easier and it will be more difficult to exhale.

Rebreathers with chest mounted breathing bags provide easy inhalation when you are swimming face down, but exhalation is usually more difficult. This occurs because you are exhaling into the breathing bag which is deeper, i.e., at a

With the breathing bag positioned
on the diver's chest, exhalation
may be more difficult when
the diver is swimming
face down.

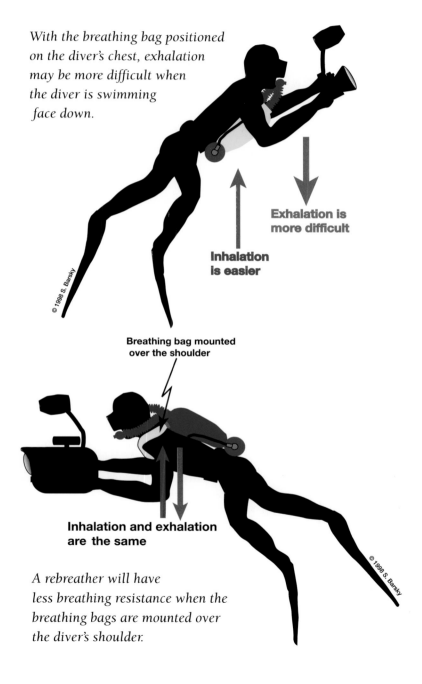

**Exhalation is
more difficult**

**Inhalation
is easier**

© 1998 S. Barsky

**Breathing bag mounted
over the shoulder**

**Inhalation and exhalation
are the same**

© 1998 S. Barsky

A rebreather will have
less breathing resistance when the
breathing bags are mounted over
the diver's shoulder.

greater pressure than your chest. If you roll onto your back, inhalation will become more difficult while exhalation will be much easier.

With the breathing bags positioned over your shoulder the breathing resistance is decreased when you are working in a head-up position. The disadvantage to having the breathing bags located here is that it can be difficult to enclose the bags in a protective shroud without creating additional bulk that can restrict the movement of your head. Bags mounted in this position can also increase your drag when you swim through the water. However, breathing bags mounted in this position provide the least breathing resistance of the three possible positions.

SHROUD

Most rebreathers are equipped with some type of shroud to cover the breathing bags, scrubber, electronics (if so equipped) and connecting plumbing. The shroud serves several purposes including mechanical protection for delicate mechanisms, streamlining, and enhancing appearance. The shroud may also serve as a framework for mounting or containing some of the hardware. For example, the bail-out bottle may be mounted on the shroud as well as the buoyancy compensator.

Most shrouds are made from either fiberglass or plastic. Either of these materials is acceptable provided the shroud is rugged enough to withstand the abuse it receives both in the water and during transport. Ideally, the shroud should be as strong as possible while still being light weight.

The shroud should be designed so that it holds all of the components of the rebreather easily without the need to cram them into the housing. Since breathing bags are flexible they will typically end up with some creases and folds in them when they are installed in the shroud. As long as the shroud does not interfere with the normal movement of the breathing bags this is acceptable.

MOUTHPIECE

When you hear divers refer to the "mouthpiece" on a rebreather, they are usually referring to the complete mouthpiece assembly which includes the actual replaceable mouthpiece, the inlet and exhaust valves, the lever, and the mouthpiece "T" where these parts all attach. There normally isn't much variation in these parts.

The inlet valve will be on the inhalation side of the "T" and the exhaust valve will be on the exhalation side. These valves are normally simple rubber "flapper" valves designed to ensure that the flow of gas goes in one direction only. They must function properly or you will end up rebreathing gas that has not gone through the scrubber.

On some rebreathers the inhalation side of the mouthpiece assembly will be on the right while on others it will be on the left. There is no standardization regarding this important issue. Each rebreather is different and you must take care if you use more than one type of rebreather to ensure that you are installing the mouthpiece in the correct orientation. In addition, some mouthpieces have an integrated bail-out regulator built directly into them.

The lever must move easily yet have enough friction that it can't be accidentally opened or closed.

The lever is designed to shut off the mouthpiece of the rebreather to prevent water from entering the system if you remove the mouthpiece while you are in the water. The lever must be large enough and move freely enough that you can operate it even when you are wearing gloves.

A lever that is too stiff will be difficult to operate, while a lever that is too loose could open or close accidentally at the wrong time. There is usually no adjustment possible on the tension required to operate the lever, although lubrication can make it easier to move it. See your dealer or instructor if you feel the lever on your rebreather is not operating properly.

HOSES

The corrugated hoses that deliver the breathing gas and transport it back to the rebreather are the most vulnerable and exposed components on the majority of rebreathers. The hoses should be kept as protected as possible.

The diameter of the hose and the smoothness of its interior bore greatly affect the breathing resistance of your system. Although there is a practical limit to how large the corrugated hoses can be, generally speaking the larger the bore of the hose the better.

Stiffeners are often placed inside the hose at the ends closest to the rebreather to help prevent the hose from collapsing under its own weight. These stiffeners are usually removable and will quite frequently fall out of the hose when you disassemble your rebreather for maintenance. Take care not to lose them.

Stiffeners are used inside the hoses to keep them from collapsing.

The hoses will also have weights on them to counteract their buoyancy due to the breathing gas inside them. One set of weights will normally be located behind you where the hoses make the connection for the breathing bags. A second set of weights will normally be positioned on the hoses a few inches either side of the mouthpiece "T".

ADDITIONAL CONSIDERATIONS

While the manual, warranty, and dealer support are not part of the rebreather itself, they are crucial items to consider when purchasing your rebreather. A good manual is essential when it comes time to maintain and service your rebreather. The best warranty program is the one you never have to depend on.

DEALER SUPPORT

Good dealer support is critical when you purchase a rebreather. Make sure that your dealer is well educated in the operation, maintenance, and repair of the rebreather you intend to buy.

Ask the dealer if he has attended the manufacturer's repair course for the models of rebreathers that he sells. Be sure that the dealer stocks the most common spare parts for your rebreather and has any special tools that are required to perform service. There is nothing worse than owning an expensive rebreather and finding out that the dealer is unable to service it.

Part of good dealer support is the support the dealer gets from the manufacturer. The best dealer will be no better than the support he gets from the factory. Even if the dealer is trained and equipped to perform service on your rebreather, he won't be able to service your system if he can't get parts from the manufacturer.

WHICH REBREATHER SHOULD YOU BUY?

If you are considering buying a rebreather you should have a specific application for the rebreather in mind. You must weigh the pros and cons of each type of rebreather to ensure it will fit your needs for the required depth, duration, and environmental conditions you will encounter during your dives. The best way to do this is to take a rebreather training course.

One of the most important aspects of rebreather selection is how the product was developed and tested. Investigate the claims made by the manufacturer. How long has the unit been in production? Who has used it? What type of diving has been done with this particular model of rebreather? How many test dives were made with prototypes before the system went into production?

Make sure the manufacturer has documentation to show how the particular model unit was tested. For example, was the canister duration tested with a light, moderate, or heavy work load? Some testing will actually combine typical operational scenarios to give a more accurate projection of how the unit will function.

Many manufacturers seek testing laboratories to check out their systems, or conduct manned and unmanned testing on their own. In some countries, government agencies may oversee certification testing and standards, or simply accept the test data from the manufacturer's own studies.

For shallow sport diving at depths not exceeding 100 feet, most divers will probably find a semi-closed circuit system will meet their needs and budget. However, if you are a technical or professional diver, you will probably be more interested in a fully closed circuit electronic rebreather.

For shallow sport diving, a semi-closed circuit system will meet the needs of most divers.

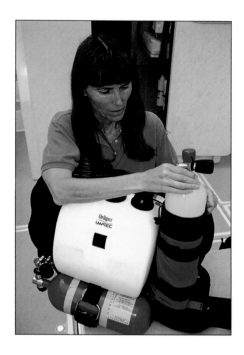

PRE-PURCHASE CHECK LIST

The following check list includes the most important items that you should consider before you purchase any rebreather.

- What is the principle of operation of the rebreather, i.e., semi-closed or fully closed circuit?
- What is the weight of the entire rebreather assembly, fully rigged, dry and in the water?
- What are the physical dimensions of the rebreather?
- What is the maximum depth at which the unit is designed to operate?
- What is the intended operational depth?
- What is the diameter of the breathing hoses?
  Bigger is generally better, but there can come a point where the hoses will restrict the movement of your head.

- What is the capacity of the scrubber, i.e., how many pounds of absorbent does it take to fill it?
- What type of absorbent material is specified for use?
- What mesh size absorbent is the unit designed to use?
- What is the canister duration in hours?
  At what temperature? At what work load?
- What is the maximum dive time the system will provide?
- What control systems are provided, i.e., oxygen monitoring, gas control, bypass functions?
- What alarm features are provided?
- What type of buoyancy control is provided?
- What type of bail-out system is provided?
- What test data is available on the performance of the system?
- Who tested the system, where and how?
- Does the system use pure oxygen?
- Who manufactured the oxygen monitoring system and electronic controls?
- What is the battery life of the system and how expensive are replacement batteries?
- What is the availability of replacement batteries?
- What computer interface abilities are present or required?
- What accessories and optional equipment are available?
- Is there a comprehensive owner's manual for the unit, that covers set-up and maintenance procedures in detail?
- How many rebreathers of this particular model have been sold?
- What type of warranty comes with the system?
- How long has the manufacturer been building this type of gear?

Knowing what features to look for when you purchase a rebreather will help ensure that you have a positive rebreather diving experience. Prior to purchasing or using a rebreather you should ask lots of questions of people who are knowledgeable in the use of these systems.

CHAPTER 4

THE HAZARDS OF REBREATHER DIVING

All diving exposes you to a certain degree of risk, whether you are snorkeling on a shallow reef in the Caribbean or inside a deep cave at a depth of 300 feet. The careful diver does everything he can to minimize these hazards, but realizes that all risk can never be completely eliminated.

Diving with a closed or semi-closed circuit rebreather poses more pitfalls than diving with ordinary open circuit scuba gear using compressed air. However, this type of equipment also offers more benefits and an extended range beyond what you can achieve using traditional diving equipment. By understanding the risks involved in using a rebreather we can help minimize these dangers and use appropriate safety precautions and back-up gear to make our diving as safe as possible. Properly prepared and equipped, the chances of a rebreather diver suffering a serious accident are small.

All of the possible problems involved in using a rebreather expose you to certain physiological risks. Some of the dangers, such as CNS (central nervous system) oxygen toxicity, can be a direct result of ignoring the depth limits for specific partial pressures of oxygen. This type of accident could also occur on open circuit scuba using air at extreme depth or using nitrox at relatively shallow depths. Oxygen toxicity problems can also occur as a result of a mistake in setting up a semi-closed circuit rebreather or through sensor failures in a fully closed circuit rebreather. No matter how these problems occur, the key is prevention rather than attempting to deal with the problem once things have gone wrong.

The direct hazards that are unique to rebreather diving include oxygen toxicity (hyperoxia), insufficient oxygen (hypoxia), carbon dioxide poisoning (hypercapnia), and chemical burns. Just trying to spell some of these hazards will be enough to scare some divers away from rebreather diving!

Of course, nitrogen narcosis can still occur with a rebreather whenever nitrogen is used as part of the breathing mix, just as it can in open circuit diving. All of the other hazards that can occur any time you dive are also possible, including ear and sinus squeeze, lung over-pressure injuries, decompression sickness, marine life injuries, drowning, shark bite and diaper rash from urinating in your wetsuit.

To use a rebreather with any degree of safety you must have a good understanding of the potential hazards of this type of equipment. Some of these hazards may give you a warning before a catastrophe occurs while others may happen with little or no warning. Knowing and recognizing the signs and symptoms of each of these hazards can mean the difference between life and death for a rebreather diver.

OXYGEN TOXICITY

There are two types of oxygen poisoning which have been identified by scientists; pulmonary oxygen toxicity and CNS oxygen toxicity. Pulmonary oxygen toxicity occurs when a person is exposed to a breathing mixture that contains an elevated partial pressure of oxygen for an extended period of time. For example, a person in an oxygen tent in a hospital can develop pulmonary oxygen toxicity. The result of this type of oxygen poisoning is primarily irritation of the lungs which makes breathing uncomfortable.

CNS oxygen toxicity occurs when a diver is exposed to a high partial pressure (pp) of oxygen (hyperoxia) at depth. For practical purposes, we will consider a ppO_2 anywhere over

1.4 as a high partial pressure of oxygen. A partial pressure of oxygen of 1.4 is the equivalent of breathing pure oxygen at a depth of approximately 13 feet. CNS oxygen toxicity is sometimes also referred to as "acute" oxygen toxicity.

Some authorities consider a ppO2 as high as 1.6 acceptable for use in rebreathers, however, we believe, based upon scientific studies, that a more conservative approach will serve both the recreational and technical diver well without imposing undue restrictions. The few extra feet of depth you gain from a higher ppO2 is not worth the risk of an oxygen convulsion. We feel a ppO2 of 1.4 is reasonable for recreational diving.

CNS oxygen toxicity can occur whether you use a semiclosed circuit rebreather or a fully closed circuit system. Although the toxic effects of oxygen under pressure will not kill you directly, an oxygen convulsion underwater could be fatal if you are by yourself and/or not wearing a full face mask.

The use of a full face mask could save your life if you suffer from an oxygen convulsion underwater.

Oxygen toxicity is caused by an excess of chemical elements known as "free radical intermediates" which are present in high concentrations when the body is exposed to oxygen at high partial pressures. These chemical elements are toxic to the body. Although the exact mechanism of oxygen poisoning is not known, presumably these toxic elements react negatively with the nervous system to produce the signs and symptoms of oxygen toxicity.

Symptoms of oxygen toxicity include visual disturbances, ringing of the ears, nausea, twitching of the lips, irritability (confusion, nervousness), and dizziness. These symptoms can be remembered by the acronym "VENTID".

V – Visual disturbances
E – Ringing of the ears and auditory hallucinations
N – Nausea
T – Twitching of the lips
I – Irritability, including anxiety, confusion, fatigue
D – Dizziness (vertigo)

However, the most serious symptom of oxygen toxicity is convulsions, which resemble those experienced by epileptics during a grand mal seizure. While it is apparent to any diver that a convulsion would be a serious event underwater, oxygen convulsions are particularly dangerous because you may get little or no warning that a seizure is about to occur. Sometimes oxygen convulsions are preceded by the symptoms listed above, but sometimes the seizure itself is the first sign that something is wrong.

If you lose your mouthpiece during an oxygen convulsion at depth there is a strong possibility that you will drown. This is one of the reasons why a full face mask is strongly recommended for rebreather diving.

Research has shown that if you do suffer from an oxygen "hit" and survive, you should have no residual effects from the convulsion itself. Of course, if you inhale water during the convulsion or suffer a lung over-pressure accident as a result of a rapid rescue effort, you will have other problems to deal with after the dive. Recovery from the convulsion itself usually takes less than five minutes after a return to air breathing.

Factors which affect the onset of oxygen toxicity include exceeding the maximum allowable depth for your mix, exceeding the maximum oxygen exposure time (either on a single dive or cumulatively), exercise, insulin exposure, and exposure to high levels of carbon dioxide. CNS oxygen toxicity is primarily determined by your exposure at depth, over time. However, if you work or swim hard, or you are an insulin dependent diabetic, or your scrubber begins to fail, you will be more prone to suffering from oxygen toxicity.

Scrubber failure is a problem that is obviously unique to rebreather divers as compared to a diver using nitrox on open circuit scuba. This is one of the reasons why you must be meticulous about recording the amount of time you have used the absorbent in your scrubber canister, and changing the absorbent in a timely manner.

Factors that affect oxygen toxicity.

The definitive research on the effects of oxygen toxicity was conducted by Dr. Kenneth Donald of the Royal British Navy. His research started in 1942 and was directly related to the use of closed circuit rebreathers by Royal Navy divers. His book, *Oxygen and the Diver*, is considered to be the definitive work on oxygen toxicity and related problems.

Dr. Donald found that there were enormous variations in a diver's tolerance to high pressure oxygen on a day-to-day basis. While a diver might tolerate a relatively high partial pressure of oxygen one day, he might experience a convulsion after a relatively short time at a shallow depth the next. The only way to reliably reduce the chances of a diver suffering from oxygen toxicity would be to limit the maximum ppO_2 to a level where almost no convulsions would occur.

Probably the most common cause of oxygen toxicity is the simplest to avoid and that is to religiously observe the depth and time limits for the gas mixture you are using. Any violation of the maximum depth limit or the time limit for your mix greatly increases your chances of suffering from oxygen toxicity.

If you are using a fully closed circuit electronic rebreather, there are several ways that oxygen toxicity can occur. First, if you have a failure of the electronics that control the oxygen level in your system and you aren't alert you could have a build-up of oxygen in the system that could cause a problem. If you accidentally flood the system with pure oxygen, or intentionally flood it with pure O_2 for decompression purposes, and are careless about your depth, this could also cause you to suffer from oxygen toxicity.

Even if someone is with you at the onset of a full blown oxygen seizure, the chances are very good that you will drown. When a person goes into an oxygen convulsion, and his body starts doing the "funky chicken", the assisting diver will have a hard time managing both divers' depths, keeping the convulsing diver at a proper attitude in the water, and maintaining the mouthpiece in place for the stricken diver. This is why a full face mask is a must for anyone diving at a ppO_2 that could pose the risk of oxygen toxicity.

Oxygen toxicity is a serious hazard that always must be kept in mind when using a rebreather. Fortunately, it is fairly easy to avoid. Don't push the limits and take chances with oxygen toxicity, thinking that you will be able to anticipate a "hit" before it occurs. You may never get any warning before you are in the clutches of an oxygen convulsion.

HYPOXIA

Hypoxia is a condition that occurs when you have too little oxygen in your breathing mixture. It can also be fatal.

Human beings have a fairly wide range of oxygen percentages that will maintain consciousness. An oxygen percentage as low as 16% is sufficient to keep a person alive, although admittedly it would be difficult for you to work very hard breathing a mixture this low in oxygen.

The symptoms of hypoxia include vision distortion (usually in the form of tunnel vision), breathlessness, tingling and dizziness, numbness in the lips, and unconsciousness. You'll note that these symptoms are very similar to those of hyperoxia (too much oxygen), so the cause of the problem may not be clear. There is usually very little time between the onset of these symptoms and unconsciousness, so you must be prepared to switch over to your bail-out system immediately at the first moment you suspect that there is a problem with your rebreather system.

There are several ways that you can be exposed to hypoxia if you are diving with a rebreather. One scenario is possible with almost all rebreathers, while the others can only occur if you are using a semi-closed circuit system.

No matter what type of rebreather you use, you can suffer from hypoxia if you forget to turn the system on prior to entering the water. Unlike open circuit scuba, where it is immediately obvious if there is no gas supplied to the regulator, with a closed circuit system you can still breathe, but you won't be getting any new oxygen. Since air is composed of 21% oxygen and we require only 16% oxygen to maintain consciousness, you can survive for one or two minutes on the air that was in the bag and your exhaled breath. However eventually, you will use up the oxygen in the breathing loop and will pass out due to hypoxia if you fail to take corrective action by opening the valve.

Never forget to turn your rebreather on before you enter the water!

If no one is near to assist you, it's almost certain you will drown if your system is not equipped with an oxygen sensor to alert you to the problem. This assumes that you will recognize why the problem is occurring and what you need to do to correct it.

With a semi-closed circuit rebreather several different unique situations can occur that could cause you to become hypoxic. These would include using an incorrect gas mixture with the wrong metering orifice, working at a high rate, and making an ascent without purging the breathing bag first. A proper pre-dive flow check will quickly identify whether you are using the correct orifice.

You can also have a problem with a semi-closed circuit rebreather if you have a defective or damaged metering nozzle that is not flowing gas at the correct rate. Manufacturers of semi-closed circuit systems normally will provide specifications for the amount of time it takes to flow a given volume of breathing gas through each of the metering nozzles included with their system. They will also usually provide you with a simple testing apparatus when you purchase your rebreather that will allow you to check the flow of gas through the system.

Manufacturers of semi-closed circuit systems normally recommend that you flow check your rig prior to every day of diving. Don't even consider buying a semi-closed circuit rebreather from a manufacturer that does not provide the gear required to accomplish a full gas flow and rig readiness check.

If you are using a semi-closed circuit rig, using a lean gas with an orifice designed to flow a rich gas mixture can lead to hypoxia. This will occur because the orifice designed to flow the rich gas will have a flow rate that can be as little as one third as fast as the flow rate of the leaner orifice. This means that you will be breathing the lean mixture for a much longer period of time and using up the available oxygen.

If you are using a semi-closed circuit system with pre-mixed gas you must be extremely careful to select the correct metered orifice for the gas mixture you are using.

Another problem with semi-closed circuit rigs is that regardless of your work level, the rebreather can only deliver the same mixture of nitrox. This is a real disadvantage if you are working heavily and consuming much of the oxygen you inhale with each breath.

At rest, our bodies use only a small amount of the percentage of oxygen that we inhale, but at high work rates, we consume more oxygen. Physiologists call this oxygen uptake or oxygen consumption, and this is an important concept that every diver who uses a semi-closed circuit unit must understand.

For example, a diver at rest may consume as little as .3 liters of oxygen per minute. At this rate of oxygen consumption, the oxygen percentage in the inhalation bag of a diver using a Dräger semi-closed circuit rebreather is 47.6% despite the 50/50 mix entering the bag from the cylinder. If the same diver works at peak capacity, the oxygen percentage in the bag can drop as low as 19.1%! Although this level of oxygen isn't low enough to cause hypoxia, leaner mixtures can put you in a precarious position if you aren't aware of the problem.

Hypoxia can also occur during ascent with a semi-closed circuit rig, as the partial pressure of each gas drops as the diver nears the surface. This can be especially dangerous if you must make an emergency ascent and you are breathing heavily.

It is extremely important to always ventilate your breathing bag several times before you make a direct ascent to the surface. This will help ensure that you have the maximum percentage of oxygen in the breathing bag before you ascend.

Always be sure to ventilate your semi-closed circuit system before making a direct ascent to the surface. Ventilate your system by exhaling through your nose.

Recovery from hypoxia is extremely rapid and occurs within minutes of breathing air or pure oxygen. There are usually no after effects from hypoxia unless you have been unconscious long enough to suffer brain damage.

An oxygen monitoring system should be a part of every rebreather to help avoid the dangers of hypoxia. Keep in mind, however, that if your oxygen monitoring system fails, for whatever reason, you may get no warning that your system is dangerously low on oxygen.

CARBON DIOXIDE POISONING

Carbon dioxide (CO_2) is the primary waste produced by our bodies as a result of breathing. A certain amount of carbon dioxide is essential in our bodies in that carbon dioxide is what triggers the stimulus to breathe. However, too much carbon dioxide in the breathing system is harmful and can lead to serious accidents. Carbon dioxide poisoning occurs when there is too much carbon dioxide (hypercapnia) in the breathing system.

The most obvious symptom of CO_2 poisoning is a feeling of breathlessness, which may also be accompanied by a severe headache. If nothing is done to solve the problem eventually the diver will black out.

The symptoms of carbon dioxide do not develop as rapidly as those of oxygen toxicity, so in many cases if you are alert, you should have the time to realize there is a problem and take action. If you start feeling as though you cannot breathe for comfort this should be a warning that you have a serious problem. The obvious solution is to immediately switch over to your bail-out supply and abort the dive.

Carbon dioxide poisoning occurs in divers whenever there are problems with the absorbent material used in the scrubber canister in rebreathers. This can happen due to physical problems with the canister itself, or through problems in the use or loading of the scrubber. It can also occur due to a failure of the valves in the mouthpiece of the rig, allowing you to rebreathe your exhaled gas from the breathing hoses without forcing it through the scrubber.

Physical problems with the canister that might cause carbon dioxide poisoning include a canister that is damaged or

improperly sealed. In either situation the main problem is water in the canister which will prevent the absorbent from functioning properly. There is also the additional danger of chemical burns that can occur when the absorbent becomes wet.

Water in your scrubber canister is a definite problem!

When a canister has been improperly loaded so that it is not tightly packed with absorbent, it is possible for your exhaled gas to move through the canister in a way that does not bring the carbon dioxide into contact with the absorbent. When this happens we say that "channeling" has occurred and CO_2 begins to build up in the system.

Absorbent that has been improperly stored, i.e., in an unsealed or loosely sealed container, will lose its moisture and absorb carbon dioxide from the air so that it is unusable for diving. This is particularly dangerous because although most absorbent turns blue (or violet) immediately after it is used, it returns to its off-white color again after another 24 hours. This means that absorbent that has been improperly stored for a long period of time will give no visual clues as to its current capabilities. If you have any doubt about the absorbent you plan to use be sure to replace it with fresh material.

Low temperatures can also prevent most CO_2 absorbents from functioning properly. Proper storage of absorbent is especially important in sub-freezing environments. Under extreme cold conditions it is essential to store absorbent at a temperature not less than 70 degrees F for 24 hours prior to diving. For diving under the ice or at near freezing temperatures it is wise to insulate the scrubber by wrapping it with neoprene to get the maximum performance from your absorbent. Absorbent efficiency is influenced by water temperature and can decrease by as much as half at temperatures of less than 40 degrees according to military tests.

Always be sure to close the lid tightly on your absorbent supply.

When the absorbent in a properly packed canister stops functioning we say that the canister has reached its "breakthrough point" and the amount of time that it takes for this to happen is its "breakthrough time". Once this happens, carbon dioxide begins to build up rapidly in the system and it is time to get out of the water.

Since it is often rare for a diver to make a single dive that uses the full capacity of his scrubber, it is not uncommon for some divers to store their partially used scrubber between dives. If you follow this practice it is essential to make sure that you carefully log the amount of time you have put on the absorbent in the canister.

Never store previously used absorbent in the original container unless the container has been marked to indicate that this is what you have done. When the absorbent reverts and loses its color change there will be no way to identify that it has already been used.

Even if you have not completely used the absorbent in your system to its capacity, if your next planned dive will exceed the maximum recommended dive time for your canister be sure to dump the contents and fill it with fresh absorbent. Never exceed the recommended dive time for your scrubber canister, either on a single dive or on cumulative shorter dives.

Some manufacturers, such as Dräger, do not recommend storing a filled canister longer than a few hours, under any conditions, whether it is used, partially used, or unused. Be sure to follow the directions provided by the manufacturer of your rebreather.

Of course, if you put no absorbent in your canister the level of carbon dioxide in the system will rise extremely rapidly. If you make a rapid descent to depth under this condition this could be a fatal mistake unless you were equipped with an open circuit bail-out system.

ASPHYXIA

Asphyxia is defined as a combination of too much carbon dioxide and not enough oxygen in the body. People who suffocate die of asphyxia.

Asphyxia can occur when you use a rebreather if the mixture you are using does not contain sufficient oxygen and your CO_2 absorbent is not performing properly. The main symptom of asphyxia is extreme shortness of breath. Unconsciousness will follow shortly.

CHEMICAL BURNS

The chemical most commonly used as the carbon dioxide absorbent in rebreathers is soda lime. Soda lime is a mixture of two chemicals, caustic soda and lime. Caustic soda is produced by combining sodium, oxygen, and hydrogen, and is designated by the chemical formula "NaOH". Lime is a combination of calcium, oxygen, and hydrogen, and is represented by the chemical formula "$Ca(OH)_2$".

When carbon dioxide passes through the granules of absorbent a chemical reaction occurs which neutralizes the acidic properties of the CO_2, liberating heat and moisture. The solid physical product that is left is chalk. However, if the absorbent is flooded when it is still chemically active, it produces a "caustic cocktail" that can cause serious burns to your body including your lips, mouth, esophagus, windpipe, and lungs.

Although most modern rebreathers have been designed with special baffle systems and/or filters to help prevent the possibility of you being injured in the event of a flooded canister, a small but real risk remains that this can occur. If you suspect that your canister has flooded, or at the first sensation of stinging in your mouth, you should immediately switch over to your bail-out supply. Divers who have first hand experience with this type of accident report that the solution feels and tastes "soapy" in your mouth.

Some rebreather manufacturers recommend the use of lithium hydroxide in their system, rather than soda lime. Be advised that lithium hydroxide is even more caustic than soda lime and can cause greater personal injury in the event your system floods.

Caustic cocktails are not something that you want to consume!

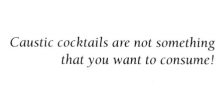

If you do suffer a chemical burn be sure to flush the affected area with plenty of fresh, clean water and see a physician immediately.

EXTREME DECOMPRESSION COMMITMENTS

Given the tremendous capabilities of closed circuit electronic rebreathers it is possible for you to dive to great depths for extended periods of time. For example, Bio-Marine advertises their BMR500 Closed Circuit Rebreather with a depth capability of 500 feet for three and a half hours. If you are not a prudent diver, Bio-Marine's rebreather, and others like it, offer a capability that is deep enough and long enough to get you in serious trouble.

Careful dive planning and appropriate back-up systems are a must for any diver using a rebreather. Using these tools we can help minimize the risks in rebreather diving, but we can never completely eliminate these risks.

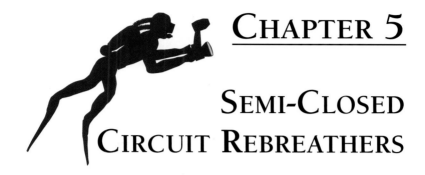

CHAPTER 5

SEMI-CLOSED CIRCUIT REBREATHERS

WARNING:

This chapter contains procedures for diving semi-closed circuit rebreathers. These procedures are for general information only, since each model of rebreather has its own specific procedures. While the principles of operation will be the same or similar for each system, use only the procedures you have been taught for your specific rebreather.

Semi-closed circuit rebreathers are probably the best type of rebreather for the average recreational diver who intends to make no-decompression dives shallower than 100 feet. For deeper diving or decompression diving, a fully closed circuit system is probably a better choice.

You may also hear semi-closed circuit rebreathers referred to as "mass flow" systems. This refers to the fact that most semi-closed circuit systems deliver a small but continuous stream of breathing gas into the breathing system. However, some semi-closed circuit systems work on a proportioning system. Like fully closed circuit rebreathers you may also hear semi-closed systems referred to as "rigs".

For depths shallower than 100 feet, nitrox is the most economical and practical breathing gas for use in a rebreather. The optimum range of the nitrox semi-closed circuit rebreather is actually down to about 70 feet where you get the greatest bottom time out of the system. Below 70 feet, the maximum bottom time shortens considerably due to the necessity of using "leaner" (i.e., less oxygen rich) mixtures with proportionally higher injection rates.

Self-mixing semi-closed circuit rebreathers have more versatility than systems that rely upon pre-mixed gas. Some of the self-mixing systems can be used with helium-oxygen mixtures down to depths of 270 FSW.

HOW MASS FLOW SEMI-CLOSED CIRCUIT SYSTEMS WORK

PRE-MIXED SYSTEMS

The breathing gas is supplied from a single or multiple cylinders to the first stage regulator. The pressure at the regulator is broken down to approximately 140 p.s.i. over the surrounding pressure. Two low pressure hoses supply gas from the first stage to both the metered orifice and the demand valve, which may be housed in the same unit. In some systems, the demand valve may be referred to as a "bypass valve", but in most cases, a bypass valve is a manually operated valve while the demand valve operates automatically.

The metered orifice supplies a constant flow of breathing gas to the breathing loop. Several different size orifices are usually available for different nitrox mixtures. As long as the supply valve at the cylinder is on, nitrox will be flowing into the system. For this reason, a semi-closed circuit rebreather is never turned on until the moment before you enter the water. If your hearing is good and you aren't wearing a hood, you will probably be able to hear the gas flowing through the metered orifice while you are diving.

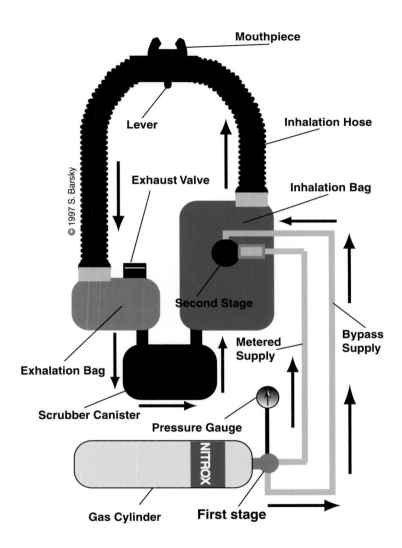

This schematic drawing shows the flow through a semi-closed circuit rebreather that uses pre-mixed nitrox.

The demand valve works in a similar fashion to a conventional open circuit second stage regulator. The demand valve senses whenever there is low volume in the breathing bag and "kicks in" supplying a surge of nitrox into the breathing bag to make up the additional volume.

Some rebreathers incorporate two separate valves; one that operates manually and another that strictly works like a demand valve to maintain breathing bag volume. The demand valve will normally operate if you make a quick descent to the bottom and get ahead of the flow of the metered orifice.

The demand valve will also flow gas whenever you clear your mask or exhale through your nose. The demand valve sounds very similar to the sound an open circuit regulator makes when you inhale. You should be able to hear the demand valve whether you are wearing a hood or not.

The manually operated valve, if the rebreather has one, operates like the valve on a water fountain. You simply press in on the valve button and the gas flows until you release it. On some rebreathers this valve is normally used when you are making a fast descent or if you want to purge the rebreather. It's called a "bypass" because the gas doesn't flow through the demand valve or metered orifice, it bypasses them.

The breathing gas from the demand valve, metered orifice, and bypass valve (if present) flow into the breathing loop on the demand, or inhalation side, of the loop. This side of the loop also receives breathing gas that has been purified in the scrubber. The gas coming into the inhalation bag from the scrubber has a lower amount of oxygen in it because this is the gas you just exhaled and it has not yet mixed with the fresh gas from the metering system. When this oxygen poor mixture combines with the fresh nitrox from the cylinder the net effect is that you end up with a mixture in the breathing bag that has a lower percentage of oxygen than what is in your nitrox cylinder.

When you inhale, the gas flows from the inhalation bag into your lungs. There is no mechanical assist with the inhalation in most rebreathers like there is in a venturi assisted open circuit regulator.

There are one way valves on either side of the mouthpiece to prevent you from inhaling your exhaled breath and your exhaled gas from going back into the inhalation bag. When you exhale, a small portion of your exhaled gas vents out through the exhaust valve in the form of very tiny bubbles. The balance of your exhalation passes into the exhalation bag, or with some rebreathers, directly into the scrubber.

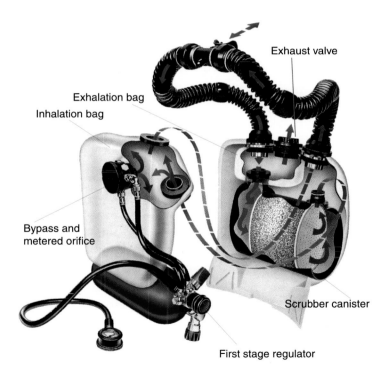

This cutaway of the Dräger Atlantis and Dolphin systems will help you have a good understanding of how this system works.

(*Courtesy of DrägerDive, Travemünde, Germany.*)

The scrubber is usually a cylindrical container that holds carbon dioxide absorbent. The absorbent removes the carbon dioxide from your exhalation and passes the oxygen depleted gas through to the inhalation bag where the purified gas mixes with fresh gas from the cylinder.

SELF-MIXING SYSTEMS

The breathing gas is supplied from two cylinders of gas. One cylinder will contain pure oxygen while the second cylinder will contain either nitrox or heliox (helium and oxygen). There is a first stage regulator on each cylinder that breaks the pressure in the cylinder down to about 140 p.s.i. over the ambient pressure.

The gas from each cylinder flows through a metered orifice that supplies a continuous stream of gas to the inhalation bag. In addition, there is a feedback system from the exhaust valve on the exhalation bag that adjusts the flow of diluent and oxygen according to the depth.

Once the gas enters the inhalation bag it mixes with the cleansed gas coming out of the scrubber. This combination of gas enters the inhalation hose where you breathe it in. There is a one way valve on each side of the mouthpiece to prevent the back flow of gas in either direction.

Dräger's M100 M is a mechanical self-mixing, semi-closed circuit rebreather. (Courtesy of DrägerDive, Travemünde, Germany.)

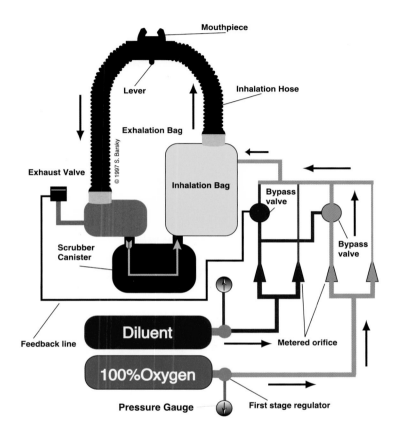

Self-mixing closed circuit rebreathers require two gas cylinders, one with pure oxygen and one with diluent.

Once you exhale, the gas goes back into the mouthpiece, through the exhalation valve, into the exhalation hose, and enters the exhalation bag. A small portion of your exhaled gas is released to the water through the exhaust valve. The exhaust valve is tied to the feedback line which controls the gas flow through the bypass valves that control the flow of oxygen and diluent.

Once the gas leaves the exhalation bag it enters the scrubber where it is purified and the carbon dioxide is removed. The gas then flows into the inhalation bag where it is available for you to breathe again.

RIGGING YOUR SYSTEM FOR DIVING

Like most diving equipment, whether you are dealing with open circuit scuba, an underwater photo system, or a rebreather, you will need to devote some time and thought to setting up your system for optimum performance. There are many different ways that you can rig your rebreather, but some arrangements work better than others. Most rebreathers are not really ready to dive as they come out of the box, but need to be configured for your bail-out, dry suit hoses, weighting, and other parameters.

Bail-out systems are essential for rebreather diving. You need to have a completely independent source of breathing gas so that in the event your rebreather fails you have another system that will supply something to breathe. In addition, you won't want to waste your breathing gas supply inflating your buoyancy compensator or dry suit and the bail-out system is used to supply these needs as well.

There are two basic ways that your bail-out can be rigged, either with an ordinary open circuit second stage or with a combination power inflator/regulator system like Scubapro's Air II or Tabata's Duo-Air Alternate Inflation Regulator. Both of these systems work well, although Tabata's unit can be fitted with a longer low pressure hose which you may need depending upon the placement of your bail-out bottle.

Using a combination power inflator/regulator allows you to eliminate an octopus rig, which will give you a much "cleaner" system. The disadvantage to this type of system is that you won't have a long hose if your dive partner needs to use your bail-out.

Tabata's Duo-Air or Scubapro's Air II will help you cut down on the number of hoses that must be used with your bail-out system.

Some systems come pre-rigged to accept a bail-out bottle while others may require the use of hose clamps or other connectors to attach a bail-out bottle to your rebreather. If your system is not pre-rigged you will need to give careful thought to how and where you mount your bail-out. You need to consider the following factors before you install a bail-out:

- How will the bail-out bottle change the balance of your system?
- Will the placement of the bail-out bottle interfere with any other equipment you are using?
- Can you reach the bail-out system if you need to turn it on or off?
- How easy is it to install or remove the bottle?
- You must ensure that the position of the bottle will not lead to entanglement with kelp, lines, nets, etc.
- Is the cylinder a sufficient size to supply something to breathe as well as gas for buoyancy control?

Generally speaking, the optimum size bail-out cylinder recommended for shallow water diving, i.e., less than 100

Your bail-out system must be rigged so that it is easy to use and will not interfere with your other equipment. Note the bail-out cylinder on the right side of the diver's body.

FSW, is 13 cubic feet. This is enough gas to allow you to adjust your buoyancy underwater and still have sufficient gas left to make a normal ascent and precautionary decompression stop in the event of a rebreather failure. For deeper dives you should consider using a larger capacity bail-out bottle.

Most semi-closed circuit rebreather divers fill their bail-out systems with compressed air rather than nitrox. If you follow this practice you should be aware that in a borderline no-decompression situation you could end up with a case of decompression sickness if you switched to your bail-out. The risk in this situation is that by switching to air you are using a leaner (less oxygen, more nitrogen) mixture that could increase the nitrogen load in your body. If you regularly dive right to the no-decompression limits you would be well advised to ensure that your bail-out bottle is set up for nitrox. Use the same mix you are using in your rebreather, or another mix that would allow you to ascend from your bottom depth and is suitable for decompression.

You may find that you need a longer than normal hose to connect to the power inflator on your buoyancy compensator, depending upon the location of your bail-out bottle. Similarly, you may need a shorter than normal hose to connect to your dry suit if your bail-out bottle is mounted on the right side of your rebreather. Your diving retailer should be able to help you secure the hoses that you need to rig your system so that you don't have hoses that are too long sticking out all over the place.

Many rebreathers are supplied with pockets in the harness provided to carry the additional weight you will need when you use the rebreather. However, the weights themselves are not normally supplied with the rebreather. How much weight you will need is primarily determined by the size of the breathing bags.

You will almost certainly need to trim out the buoyancy of your rebreather with some additional weights.

Your instructor will be able to give you insights into how much additional weight you need. You may find that your needs may be slightly different, so don't be afraid to experiment if you feel you are either too heavy or too light. Make gradual changes of a pound at a time per dive rather than making one large change.

Many rebreathers are equipped with weights to control the buoyancy of the breathing hoses near the mouthpiece. The placement of these weights on the breathing hoses greatly influences the comfort of your mouthpiece while you dive. Individual divers have quite different needs when it comes to the placement of these weights.

The closer the weights are to the mouthpiece, the heavier the mouthpiece will feel in your mouth. The further the weights are from the mouthpiece, the lighter the mouthpiece will feel in your mouth. An improperly adjusted mouthpiece can cause a great deal of discomfort on a dive, so be sure to take the time to adjust the weights for your individual needs. Most smaller divers will generally prefer a mouthpiece that feels a bit lighter, while most larger divers will usually want the mouthpiece to feel a bit heavier.

The weights can be slid along the corrugated hose to the proper position while you are underwater. However, not everyone is able to do this by themselves underwater due to the angle at which you must bend your arms to slide your weights. If you are diving with another rebreather diver you should alert them to the fact that you may need them to adjust your weights while you are underwater so they will understand what it is you want them to do when you signal them.

The exhaust valve on a semi-closed circuit system must also be adjusted for your individual breathing comfort. Most systems use a dry suit style of exhaust valve. Turn the valve

Don't be afraid to move the weights on the breathing hoses until the mouthpiece is "balanced" for your comfort. The mouthpiece should feel neither too buoyant nor too heavy.

"in", i.e., clockwise and you will find the breathing resistance of the system will increase and it will become more difficult to exhale. Turn the valve "out", i.e., counterclockwise and you will find the breathing resistance will decrease and exhalation will be much easier. If the valve is opened all the way you will use your breathing gas at a very rapid rate because the demand valve will be activated frequently.

Small divers will normally find that they will need the exhaust valve to be open more than a larger diver will. With their smaller lung volume, they can have a difficult time exhaling if the exhaust valve is not open enough. With the exhaust valve open further the breathing bags will not be as full. One of the positive aspects of this is that the buoyancy of the system will not be as great, allowing the smaller diver to use less weight.

Very large divers may find that they can dive with the exhaust valve almost completely closed. Again, your dive partner must understand how to properly adjust your exhaust valve, particularly if it is positioned behind you where you can't reach it. If your valve is not properly set when you enter the water your buddy needs to understand how to adjust it for you.

Selecting the appropriate dive computer is also essential if you want to get

Be sure to set the exhaust valve at a back-pressure that works best for you. Smaller divers will need the exhaust valve open more than larger divers.

the most out of your semi-closed circuit rebreather. Ideally, your dive computer should track the oxygen percentage in your breathing bag to give you an accurate picture of both your decompression status as well as your CNS oxygen level. Without a dive computer that performs both these functions, you are stuck making a choice of which parameter is more important and setting your computer accordingly.

Most rebreather divers find that using a snorkel is uncomfortable with the double hose system used on the rebreather and depend on their rebreather for surface swimming. This is acceptable provided you have included the time of the surface swim in your dive plan. In fact it's usually recommended that you not remove the mouthpiece at any time while you are in the water to avoid the possibility of introducing water into the rebreather. You can carry a snorkel with you in the event you need it, but it's generally easier to use the rebreather, or swim on your back if you are out of breathing gas.

PRE-DIVE PREPARATION

GAS SELECTION

As previously mentioned, one of the drawbacks of diving with a semi-closed circuit diving system is that you must make a decision about what depth range you will dive in before you leave for your dive trip. Since these rebreathers use metered orifices there is no precise adjustment of your mix. While this might seem like a serious disadvantage, most divers usually will have some idea about the depths they will be diving prior to their departure.

Semi-closed circuit units that use pre-mixed gas will normally be supplied with several different metering orifices. Typical gas mixes that will be utilized by these types of systems might include 60% nitrox, 50% nitrox, and 40% nitrox. You must decide what gas mixture you intend to use when you go to the dive shop to have your cylinder filled.

With a semi-closed circuit diving system, the richer the gas mixture you select, the longer your gas cylinder will last. This is due to the fact that these rebreathers use a slower flow rate for richer gas mixtures. For example, on the Dräger Atlantis and Dolphin system a 30 cubic foot cylinder filled with 60% oxygen/40% nitrogen will give you 121 minutes of bottom time at depths down to 50 FSW. However, the same cylinder filled with 40% oxygen/60% nitrogen will only give you 67 minutes of bottom time at depths down to 98 FSW.

The following table, Table 5-1, provides a breakdown of the maximum dive times provided using a 30 cubic foot cylinder with the Dräger Dolphin and Atlantis systems. Unlike open circuit scuba, where you consume more gas the deeper you dive, the semi-closed circuit rebreather's gas usage is "constant" regardless of the depth, for a particular gas mixture. This is one of the major advantages of using a rebreather.

Note that this table is based upon a maximum partial pressure of oxygen (ppO_2) of 1.5 for depths down to 65 FSW. Many training agencies use a more conservative limit of 1.4, while some groups use a more liberal ppO_2 of 1.6.

With the Dräger Atlantis and Dolphin systems, using mixtures containing 40% oxygen and 32% oxygen, the ppO_2 at the maximum depth is almost 1.6. You should be extremely conservative using these mixtures at their maximum depth limits, particularly if you anticipate that you may end up working hard. Heavy work loads and maximal ppO_2s are not compatible and can lead to oxygen convulsions underwater. An oxygen "hit" at depth is usually a fatal event.

The times listed in the table are independent of your dive depth. These are not no-decompression limits; they are the approximate dive times that you can expect the 30 cubic foot cylinder to last. However, if your exhaust valve is not adjusted correctly or you clear your mask frequently you will lose gas from the system and your dive duration will be considerably shorter. Note that the amount of dive time provided by mixtures containing 40% oxygen and 32% oxygen exceed the no-decompression limits for the maximum depths at which you can use these mixtures.

TABLE 5-1: GAS SELECTION TABLE FOR DRÄGER DOLPHIN AND ATLANTIS SEMI-CLOSED CIRCUIT REBREATHERS

Mixture	Maximum Depth Limit	Approximate Gas Duration[1]
60% Oxygen/40% Nitrogen	50 FSW**	121 minutes
50% Oxygen/50% Nitrogen	65 FSW**	96 minutes
40% Oxygen/60% Nitrogen	98 FSW***	67 minutes*
32% Oxygen/68% Nitrogen	130 FSW***	45 minutes*

1: Based upon a 30 cubic foot cylinder.
*Note: These times exceed the no-decompression limits for these depths!
** Based upon a ppO2 of 1.5.
*** Based upon a ppO2 of 1.6.

You must always plan to use the "richest" mixture possible for the maximum depth you will attain on any given dive. Keeping this in mind, you must not exceed the cut-off depth for the mixture you are using.

At rest, the average person normally consumes about .3 liters (.01 cubic feet) of oxygen per minute. At a low-to-moderate work load, swimming at a relaxed rate along a reef, your oxygen consumption will rise to about 1.0 liter (.03 cubic feet) of oxygen per minute. Divers who are in peak physical condition, working very hard underwater, might be able to consume as much as 2.5 liters (.09 cubic feet) of oxygen per minute. However, even very fit divers could not sustain this rate of effort for more than a few minutes at most.

Changes in your oxygen consumption will affect the level of oxygen in the inhalation bag in your semi-closed circuit system. With very high work loads, the oxygen level, even with the richest gas mixture, can actually drop below 21%, which is the normal amount of oxygen in air. Swimming against a one knot current underwater is much harder work and consumes more oxygen than sitting on the bottom taking underwater photos. Realistically, however, most people cannot maintain a high work load for more than a few minutes.

The harder you work during a dive, the more oxygen your body consumes and this will directly affect the oxygen level in the breathing bag. When you are working hard, your body uses more of the oxygen you inhale with each breath, rather than returning it to the system. The minimum percentage of oxygen required to maintain consciousness at the surface is 16%.

Sustained heavy work loads should never be attempted when using most rebreathers, unless the system is specifically designed to handle this type of demand and proper back-up systems are in place. Performing heavy work while you are free swimming with a rebreather can be dangerous. For this reason, in the military world, when rebreathers are used for deep work they are umbilical supplied. They generally have the additional support of hot water to the diver for maintaining body temperature and to the scrubber canister, along with a full helmet, communications and redundant back-up gas supplies.

Table #5-2 was developed by Dräger and shows the oxygen percentage you can expect in your inhalation bag with different gas mixtures and work loads. This table is the result of extensive testing at the Dräger lab. If your rebreather does not have an integrated dive computer that constantly monitors the percentage of oxygen in the breathing bag, you must plan your dive based upon your highest anticipated oxygen consumption. If this is not done, your decompression calculations could be wrong, causing you to suffer from decompression sickness.

TABLE 5-2: OXYGEN PERCENTAGE
IN THE INHALATION BAG OF
DRÄGER ATLANTIS AND DOLPHIN SYSTEMS
BASED UPON VARYING WORK LOADS

Gas Mixture	Oxygen Consumption by the Diver	Oxygen Percentage in the Inhalation Bag
60% Oxygen/40% Nitrogen	.3 liters /minute	57.4%
	1.0 liters/minute	49.9%
	1.5 liters/minute	42.6%
	2.5 liters/minute	19.2%
50% Oxygen/50% Nitrogen	.3 liters/minute	47.6%
	1.0 liters/minute	41.0%
	1.5 liters/minute	35.1%
	2.5 liters/minute	19.1%
40% Oxygen/60% Nitrogen	.3 liters/minute	38.0%
	1.0 liters/minute	32.9%
	1.5 liters/minute	28.8%
	2.5 liters/minute	18.6%
32% Oxygen/68% Nitrogen	.3 liters/minute	30.5%
	1.0 liters/minute	26.8%
	1.5 liters/minute	23.9%
	2.5 liters/minute	17.4%

All things being equal, you should select the richest gas mixture that is appropriate for your working depth. This will help ensure that you have the highest possible percentage of oxygen in your breathing bag. In practical terms, even though you can use a mixture containing 32% oxygen at a depth of 40 feet, you will be better off if you use a mixture containing 60% oxygen at this depth to optimize the benefits of nitrox. This will also provide a lower gas flow, which will allow you a longer total dive time.

GAS ANALYSIS

If you did not analyze your cylinder when you picked it up at the dive store it is essential to check the oxygen percentage prior to diving. The percentage of oxygen, the cylinder pressure, and the date the cylinder was filled should all be marked on the nitrox tag attached to the cylinder, if you are using a system with pre-mixed gas.

If you are using a self-mixing system, you will have two cylinders of gas, one filled with pure oxygen, and one filled with diluent.

Always check the percentage of oxygen in your cylinder yourself prior to diving with your rebreather!

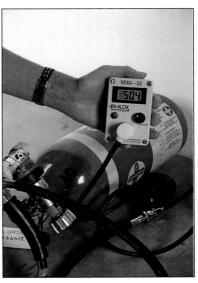

PACKING THE SCRUBBER CANISTER

Your scrubber canister should be packed as close in time as possible to when you dive. Ideally, it should be filled just before you get in the water, but realistically this isn't always possible, particularly if you are diving out of a small boat like an inflatable. It's a generally accepted practice to pack your canister the night before a dive trip if you plan to dive the next day.

To avoid getting absorbent dust in your home or garage it's a good idea to fill your scrubber canister outdoors. Put a clean drop cloth or tarp underneath your canister on the ground in the location where you intend to fill it. Place your canister on the tarp and pour the absorbent into the canister from a height of at least a foot or two above the canister. This will allow absorbent dust to be carried away by the wind rather than entering the canister where it can be inhaled. Dispose of unused absorbent dust according to the manufacturer's directions. Rinse the tarp thoroughly with fresh water when you are done.

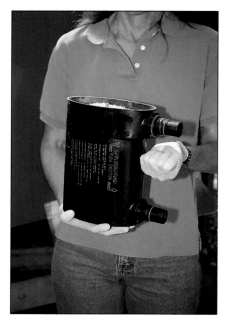

> **WARNING:**
> **Absorbent dust**
> **is caustic and**
> **can cause**
> **chemical burns.**

Tap the side of the canister to help settle the absorbent. This will help prevent channeling.

Fill the canister a bit at a time and tap the sides of the canister to ensure that it is packed tightly with no gaps. If the absorbent isn't packed tightly in the canister this can lead to "channeling", where the exhaust gas passes through the scrubber without coming into full contact with the chemical absorbent. If this happens you can get a very rapid carbon dioxide build-up in the system, which could cause you to black out underwater.

Once your canister is filled be sure to close the lid of the container of absorbent tightly. If the absorbent container is exposed to the open air without a lid, over time it will react with the carbon dioxide in the air and will no longer be effective. Although many absorbents have a chemical indicator that turns violet once it is spent, the indicator will lose its color after 24 hours and the absorbent will appear to be "fresh". If the absorbent is not violet there is no way to tell whether it is usable or not. If there is the slightest doubt whether a batch of absorbent is fresh or not, it must be discarded.

Once your scrubber is filled be sure to seal it properly. If your scrubber is transparent you will be able to see inside and know whether any of the absorbent is shifting around when you shake it, indicating it is not packed properly. If your scrubber is not transparent, shake the scrubber and listen to hear whether there is loose absorbent shifting back and forth inside. If the canister is not tightly packed remove the lid and add more absorbent until it reaches the proper level. Test it again to make sure there is no movement of absorbent inside.

Any time your loaded rebreather has been subjected to vibration, such as a long bumpy ride in a car or on a boat, it's a good idea to check the canister for settling. A canister can pack itself tightly when subject to long, steady vibrations. Some manufacturers use a spring-loaded plate to help keep the canister contents tightly packed.

Shake the canister and listen for the sound of loose absorbent.

Seal the outlet side of the scrubber canister with your palm and try to blow through the canister. You should not be able to hear any gas escaping from the canister. If gas is escaping, remove the lid, locate the leak, and reseal it.

Never dive with a leaking scrubber canister. If gas can get out, water can get in. If this happens you will be exposed to the notorious "caustic cocktail" which results when scrubber absorbent mixes with water. This solution can cause serious chemical burns to your skin, lips, mouth, throat, windpipe, and lungs. If you are exposed to this caustic mixture it is essential that you flush your skin, mouth and lips with fresh water and seek a doctor's attention immediately.

Seal the outlet side of the canister with your hand and attempt to blow through it. You must not hear any air escaping from the canister.

PRE-DIVE ASSEMBLY AND INSPECTION

Each different rebreather has a different assembly method. It is essential that you follow the exact method for putting your system together that is recommended by the manufacturer. However, certain techniques are considered universal for all rebreathers, such as inspecting all of the components prior to assembly and making sure the breathing bags and hoses are free of any debris or contaminants.

Never overtighten any of the fittings on your system. Unless special tools are recommended for assembling your rebreather, never tighten any of the connections with a pliers, vice grips, or wrench.

Just as a skydiver always packs his own parachute, you should always set up your own rebreather; never let someone else do it for you. It is helpful though to have your rebreather diving partner watch you while you set up your system so they can double check your assembly.

Never hurry through the assembly of your rebreather. Take your time and be methodical. Stop once you have assembled the system and inspect your work to make sure you haven't done something improperly. If your manufacturer hasn't supplied a checklist for proper assembly you should develop your own to ensure that you have followed all of the essential steps.

For most semi-closed circuit rebreathers the sequence of assembly will include:

- Analyzing the gas mixture.
- Connecting the gas cylinder.
- Testing the flow rate of the selected orifice.
- Testing the non-return valves in the hoses.
- Filling the scrubber canister.
- Attaching the breathing bag(s) to the canister.
- Test the demand valve (bypass valve).
- Installing the breathing bag(s) and canister in the shroud.

- Connecting the bypass (demand valve) and metered orifice to the inhalation bag.
- Attaching the breathing hoses.
- Connecting the gas cylinder(s).
- Testing the assembled system.
- Submerge the system in a container of fresh water to check for leaks.

All rebreathers have a non-return valve on either side of the mouthpiece that must be tested prior to assembling the unit. To test the inhalation valve in the mouthpiece, place the open end of the inhalation hose up to your mouth, seal it against your lips, and attempt to suck air through the hose. You should not be able to get any air back through the hose.

To test the exhalation valve in the mouthpiece, place the open end of the exhalation hose up to your mouth, seal it against your lips, and attempt to blow air through the hose. You should not be able to blow any air back through the hose.

Test the inhalation and exhalation valves in the mouthpiece.

Your individual model of rebreather may require a slightly different assembly sequence, so be sure to follow the sequence recommended by the manufacturer and taught by your instructor. Nothing about the assembly should be particularly difficult, but it must be done correctly. Diving with an improperly assembled rebreather can kill you.

Depending upon the type of rig you are using, your bail-out system may need to be set up either before or after you have set up your rebreather, or it may not matter. Consult the owner's manual of your rebreather to see what is recommended.

Your bail-out cylinder must be full at the start of each dive. Once you have attached the regulator, check the cylinder pressure and test the second stage to be sure that it is working properly.

Always be sure to check the cylinder pressure in your bail-out bottle prior to diving with your rebreather.

TESTING YOUR REBREATHER

There are several different tests that should be performed prior to each day of diving with your rebreather. These include a flow test, a negative pressure leak test. You should also test the demand valve by attempting to inhale through it. Each one of these tests is essential.

FLOW TESTING

The flow test is used to determine whether or not you are getting the correct flow through the metered orifice of your rebreather. Each one of the metered orifices should flow gas at a specific rate that is determined by the manufacturer. The richer the gas mixture (i.e., more oxygen) the slower the flow rate will be, while the leaner (i.e., less oxygen) the mixture, the faster the flow rate.

For each individual metered orifice there is a range of time within which the rebreather must flow a certain volume of breathing gas. If the rebreather doesn't flow enough gas during that time period you could end up with a very lean mixture in your breathing system. If this happens, and you do not have an oxygen monitoring meter connected to your rebreather to alert you to the problem, you could end up suffering from decompression sickness if you are diving your rebreather based upon the nitrox dive tables or dive computer. In a worst case scenario, you could end up with hypoxia and pass out from a lack of oxygen.

If the flow through the metered orifice is too fast, you would go through your gas supply very quickly. It is probably more common for a metered orifice to become plugged with corrosion, or other debris, and flow gas at too slow a rate rather than for it to flow gas at too high a rate.

Most rebreather manufacturers will provide you with some type of simple test apparatus to ensure that the metered orifice is providing the proper flow rate. For example, the test apparatus that Dräger uses for the Atlantis and Dolphin systems consists of a plastic bag with a connection for the bypass and metered orifice on one side and a tube with a one way flapper valve on the other. The test bag is connected to the bypass and metered orifice and the tube is filled with water. Once the test bag is full, the gas pressure must overcome the weight of the water in the tube before it can escape through the flapper valve. It will do this with a fairly rapid "burp" of water that will shoot several inches into the air.

The amount of time it takes to fill the bag and have the water burp out of the tube must be within a range of values

Connect the test bag to the orifice for the second stage.

Squeeze all of the air out of the bag.

Fill the tube with water up to the line inside the tube.

Turn the gas on and time how long it takes to fill the bag, making the water "burp" out of the top of the tube. Check the time against the table of acceptable values from your owner's manual.

for each metered orifice. The gas flow through a semi-closed circuit rebreather is not a precise thing; it can actually fall within a fairly broad range of times. However, if it falls outside these times this indicates there is a problem.

An improper flow rate could be caused by a number of problems. First, double check your gas mix. If you mistakenly grabbed the wrong nitrox cylinder for the metered orifice you have selected, it will not have the proper flow rate for the dive you are planning and will definitely throw things off. Next, make sure you have installed the proper metering orifice for the mix you are using.

If you have the correct tools and gauge, you can try checking the intermediate pressure supplied by the first stage regulator, if you know its correct setting. It's possible for the first stage to "creep" to a higher pressure, or fall to a lower pressure if the unit has not been serviced in a while or there is foreign matter in the regulator.

It's a good idea to keep a log on your rebreather to track the flow values for your system. If you see that the flow rate is gradually changing over a period of use you will be alerted to a potential problem before your rig gets to the point where you are unable to use it. In your log you should also track the first stage pressure as well.

If you are unable to locate the source of the problem and correct it, you must have your rebreather serviced by a trained technician. Do not use your rebreather if the flow rate does not fall within the acceptable range for the specific orifice and gas mixture you are using.

Check the owner's manual for your rebreather to verify the exact procedure for your system.

NEGATIVE PRESSURE LEAK TEST

Once you have completely assembled your rebreather, you must test it to ensure there are no leaks. The test is very simple; merely place the mouthpiece in your mouth, open the lever, and inhale as fully as possible. The breathing bags will collapse as you inhale. Close the lever before you exhale or remove the mouthpiece from your mouth.

Watch the breathing bags for at least 30 seconds to ensure that they do not reinflate, which would indicate a leak. If there is a leak you must locate it before you can dive.

Leaks can occur any number of places - in the breathing bags, the hoses, the fittings, or the scrubber canister. Check all the fittings to make sure they are tightly closed. Check the bags and hoses to ensure there are no punctures. Recheck the scrubber to make sure that it is properly sealed.

Even if you assembled your rebreather at home and performed a leak test there you should still perform another negative pressure leak test once you arrive at the dive site. The vibration of a boat or car trip can cause fittings to loosen, creating a leak.

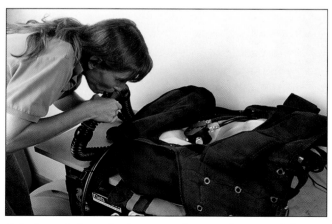

Inhale and close the lever on the mouthpiece while you are still inhaling.

Watch the bag for at least 30 seconds to make sure no air is leaking back into the system. The bags must not reinflate by themselves.

POSITIVE PRESSURE LEAK TEST

As a double check to ensure that there is no leakage you should also perform the positive pressure leak test. To do this test you will need a five pound diving weight and your rebreather, which must be completely assembled.

Place your rebreather on a level, stable surface, with the breathing bags accessible. Close the exhaust valve on your rebreather all the way. Most semi-closed circuit units use a dry suit exhaust valve which is closed by turning the head of the valve clockwise.

Open the cylinder valve until the breathing bags are completely full and then close the cylinder valve. The bags should be very firm when the system is completely filled with breathing gas. Place the five pound weight on top of the breathing bag and note the time. The bag should not noticeably deflate within 30 seconds.

If the bag sinks within 30 seconds under the force of the weight this indicates there is a leak. Do not dive until you find the source of the leak and correct the problem. The most reliable way to perform a leak test is to submerge your rebreather, with the gas turned on, in a tub of clear, clean water.

The positive pressure leak test is best performed on dry land, rather than on a rocking boat. If sea conditions are rough, the weight will slide around and it will not be possible to get a good test. In addition, if the weight slips off the bag it could cause personal injury or damage to your equipment.

Don't forget to reset the exhaust valve at the completion of this test. If the valve is closed all the way you will find that breathing is extremely difficult with the rebreather.

Close the exhaust valve all the way to perform the positive pressure leak test.

Turn on the gas, fill the bag, turn the gas off and place a five pound weight on top of the breathing bag.

Observe the bag for 30 seconds. It must not deflate under the pressure of the weight.

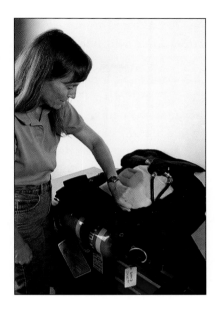

You can also test your rebreather by turning the gas on, closing the mouthpiece, and submerging it in a tub of water and looking for leaks. The only place where gas should be escaping is through the exhaust valve. This is the most accurate way to identify whether your system is leaking or not.

DIVE PLANNING

One of the most important aspects of dive planning with a semi-closed circuit rebreather involves planning your oxygen exposure and calculating your no-decompression time or decompression obligation. Whether you use a dive computer or not, you must understand what your exposure will be.

CALCULATING YOUR CNS OXYGEN EXPOSURE

Even if your semi-closed circuit rebreather is equipped with a state-of-the-art oxygen sensor system, you must still always do the math and determine your maximum cut-off depth and ppO_2 exposure time for the mixture you are using. This is essential in the event that you lose your oxygen monitoring ability so you know where you are in regards to your maximum oxygen exposure time.

An oxygen monitoring capability with a semi-closed circuit system will help you know whether your ppO2 is low or high. This is especially helpful if your ppO2 is low and you are working at a high rate or making an ascent. A monitoring system will also let you know if your ppO2 is too high because you have exceeded your cut-off depth. However, when making your calculations, you must assume that you are being exposed to the full percentage of oxygen available in the cylinder, even though you know that the percentage of oxygen in the inhalation bag will be lower during the dive.

As technology moves forward there are promises of new computers and oxygen sensor packages that will surely make all rebreather diving much safer and more efficient. If you already own a semi-closed circuit rebreather it would benefit you to have an oxygen monitoring capability.

Whenever you are nitrox diving, whether it is with a rebreather or open circuit, be sure to allow yourself a minimum 90 minute surface interval between dives to allow the CNS level of oxygen in your body to decrease. Most training agencies also recommend no more than three nitrox dives during any single day. Of course, you should never exceed the maximum total exposure to oxygen for a given partial pressure during any 24 hour day.

In addition, it is recommended that you never let your CNS oxygen exposure rise above 80%. If it reaches this level, you should stay out of the water for a minimum of two hours.

Always keep in mind that even when you stay within the limits of the CNS exposure tables the possibility exists that you could still fall victim to a CNS convulsion. All it takes is for you to have an "off" day; a day when things aren't quite right with your body. There have been documented cases where divers have had episodes of CNS toxicity at a ppO2 of less than 1.3, with exposure times well within what is considered a "safe" exposure.

Always allow a minimum 90 minute surface interval between nitrox dives!

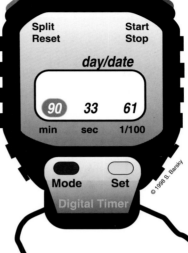

CALCULATING YOUR DECOMPRESSION OBLIGATION

The simplest method of calculating your decompression is to use a dive computer that is integrated with your rebreather and that senses the percentage of oxygen in your breathing bag. This type of computer will give you both your correct decompression obligation and your CNS oxygen level.

Semi-closed circuit rebreathers did not use oxygen sensors in the past due to reliability issues. Some divers view this lack of dependence on electronics as an asset. By combining sophisticated dive computers and oxygen monitoring with a mechanical semi-closed circuit rebreather you can have the reliability of a mechanical system with real time oxygen monitoring, decompression calculations, and CNS exposure time. This can help make diving safer.

If you have a nitrox dive computer that you intend to use with your rebreather, the first thing you must do is to ensure that you can program it for the percentage of oxygen you will be using. Next, you must make a decision whether to set the computer to calculate your maximum CNS oxygen exposure, or your decompression. Most computers won't allow you to do both. If you set the computer for the percentage of oxygen in your cylinder, your decompression may be seriously compromised. If you set the computer for the level of oxygen you have calculated for your breathing bag, then your CNS oxygen exposure may be incorrect. This is a real dilemma because it's simply not possible to rely solely upon one nitrox computer for both calculations.

Probably the simplest answer is to set your dive computer for the minimum oxygen you anticipate having in your breathing bag and use the computer for your decompression calculations. Use the CNS oxygen exposure tables you got during your nitrox course to calculate your oxygen exposure based upon the contents of your cylinder. Since computing oxygen exposure is fairly straightforward, i.e., check your mix against your depth to get your CNS exposure.

Standard nitrox dive computers are not designed for use with a rebreather. They do not compute the changes in oxygen level that occur in the breathing bag during the dive and thus cannot give an accurate picture of both CNS oxygen levels and decompression.

Some divers set their nitrox dive computers for the level of oxygen they assume to be in their breathing bag and use this percentage for both decompression and CNS tracking. While you might get away with this for awhile, you are taking a risk with both your decompression and your CNS oxygen exposure.

If you do not have a nitrox dive computer, but you still want to base your allowable bottom time on nitrox no-decompression limits, you will need to calculate your inspired percentage of oxygen, i.e., what's in your breathing bag. To calculate your inspired oxygen you will need to know the following information:

- The cylinder oxygen percentage or "Cylinder O_2%"
- The flow rate used by your rebreather, in cubic feet per minute. This information comes from your rebreather manual. It is specific as to which metered orifice you are using. Be careful to note whether the data supplied is listed in liters per minute or cubic feet per minute. Your calculations must use consistent measures throughout.
- The volume of oxygen, or "VO_2", you consume
  This figure is the least reliable since we have no way of knowing your actual VO_2. We must make some assumptions in this regards. To be conservative, we will assume a high VO_2. Again be careful to use the same units of measure that you used for the flow rate; i.e., either liters per minute or cubic feet per minute.

The formula used to compute what's in your breathing bag is shown here.

Inspired percentage of oxygen=

$$\frac{(\text{Cylinder } O_2\% \text{ X Flow Rate}) - VO_2}{(\text{Flow Rate } - VO_2)}$$

As an example, let's compute the inspired percentage of oxygen based upon these assumptions:

- Your cylinder is filled with 50% oxygen/50% nitrogen.
- The flow rate of your rebreather's metered orifice for this mixture is .35 cubic feet per minute (or 9.91 liters). (Based upon the flow rate from your rebreather manual.)
- Your oxygen consumption rate (VO_2) is .05 cubic feet per minute or (1.42 liters per minute). (Based upon a moderate swim rate.)

Inspired percentage of oxygen= $\dfrac{(.50 \text{ X } .35) - .05}{(.35-.05)}$ = 41.6%

Metric calculations: $\dfrac{(.50 \text{X} 9.91) - 1.42}{(9.91-1.42)}$ = 41.6%

Inspired percentage of oxygen= 42% (rounded up)

Based upon this example, you would make your decompression calculations based upon 42% oxygen in the breathing bag. If your exact oxygen percentage is not given in the tables you are using, select the next lower oxygen percentage listed. It's better to be conservative with your decompression and assume a lower percentage of oxygen than to try to maximize your bottom time based upon an incorrect assumption.

If you want to be ultra-conservative, you can make all of your rebreather dives according to an air diving table or air diving dive computer. This technique is used by many nitrox divers and is very simple. Of course, you will still need to track your CNS oxygen exposure based upon the percentage of oxygen in your cylinder.

DONNING YOUR REBREATHER

Donning a rebreather is almost identical to donning an ordinary open circuit system. However, with most rebreathers there will be more hoses and gauges that must be properly routed and connected.

If you have been on a long boat ride (more than an hour) to get to the dive site, take a moment to double check all of the fittings on your rebreather to make sure they are still snug. Your gear may have shifted on deck during the trip, or vibrations from the boat can cause fittings to loosen up.

Always take a moment to double check that all fittings are tight prior to donning your equipment. It's not uncommon for fittings to loosen during a long, rough boat trip.

You may find it's easier to leave your bail-out bottle and nitrox cylinder separate from your rebreather while you are transporting it. If this is the case, you will obviously need to install these items prior to diving. Be sure to check the pressure in the bail-out bottle and test the bail-out regulator prior to entering the water.

Double check the setting for your exhaust valve. The breathing resistance of these systems is determined largely by the setting of the exhaust valve. It's important to find a setting that provides a comfortable exhalation pressure yet allows sufficient volume to remain in the breathing bags to accommodate your tidal volume. Conversely, failure to maintain a sufficient exhaust pressure will cause more frequent activation of the bypass and wastes breathing gas.

*Double check
the setting for
your exhaust
valve.*

*Always use a bail-out bottle
with your semi-closed circuit
system.*

*Connect the bail-out regulator
and test it before you enter the
water.*

While most rebreathers are not much heavier than ordinary open circuit scuba, they tend to be a bit bulkier by the time you add on a bail-out system and buoyancy compensator. For this reason, it is generally easier and safer to have your dive partner assist you in donning your rebreather. He can either hold the system up for you while you slip into it or stabilize the rig while it sits on a rail or a bench on the boat as you slide into the straps.

Have your dive partner assist you in donning your rebreather.

Once you have your rebreather on, be sure to take the time to carefully position your hoses and ensure that they are properly connected. Any connections that cross your chest must be easily released in the event that you need to ditch your system.

Do not turn your rebreather on until the last moment before you enter the water. Check your submersible pressure gauge, or integrated dive computer, to ensure your cylinder is full and turned on. You should be able to hear the gas flowing through the system and escaping through the exhaust valve.

As mentioned previously, you must never forget to open the cylinder valve before you start your dive. Failure to do so could lead you to suffer from hypoxia and black-out.

Although divers using pure oxygen rigs or closed circuit rigs with helium-oxygen mixtures will avoid contaminating their rebreathers with nitrogen by exhaling before they put the mouthpiece in their mouths, this isn't necessary with a nitrox system. Simply place the mouthpiece in your mouth and inhale.

Always be sure to turn your rebreather on before entering the water.

WATER ENTRY AND DESCENT

You may enter the water by any of the normal means that you would use to dive, including both front and back rolls as well as giant strides. Any of these methods is acceptable and will not affect the performance of your rebreather.

Once you have entered the water and submerged a few feet, you and your dive partner should check each other for leaks from your rebreathers. As you make your feet first descent, spin 360 degrees so that your partner can look over your system to ensure that you aren't losing any breathing gas. Check your partner's system for leaks as well.

As you descend you should be monitoring your rebreather to ensure that it is functioning properly. Listen for the sound of the gas flowing through the metered orifice. You should also be able to hear the sound of the demand valve as it kicks in and adds gas to the system during your descent. Look at your submersible pressure gauge occasionally to see that the pressure is dropping which will also confirm that gas is flowing through the system.

Have your partner check your system for leaks as soon as you descend a few feet.

With some rebreather systems, depending upon how the shroud is constructed and where the breathing bags are placed, you will also be able to feel the movement of the breathing bags as they follow your inhalations and exhalations. As a well trained rebreather diver you don't need to monitor your rebreather continuously, but you must be attuned to any changes in the performance of your system and take notice of them the moment something is not right.

DURING THE DIVE

During the dive you will find that your rebreather should become almost unnoticeable. The difference in the noise level between using the rebreather and diving with open circuit equipment is dramatic.

Your buoyancy must be adjusted underwater by using either your buoyancy compensator, or your dry suit if you are wearing one. Exhaling to make yourself sink does not work with a rebreather because the gas just circulates around the breathing loop, with no change of buoyancy.

Try to avoid clearing your mask or exhaling through your nose any more than is absolutely necessary during the course of the dive. Every time that you exhale through your nose you will lose gas that could have been recirculated and you will decrease your bottom time.

If you find yourself working very hard for a sustained period, you should periodically purge your breathing system by inhaling through your mouth and exhaling through your nose until you hear the demand valve kick in. This will give an instantaneous refill to the breathing bag and raise the ppO_2 back up.

Monitor yourself during the dive to ensure that you are not experiencing either a CO_2 build-up or hypoxia. Either one of these situations could lead to a fatal accident.

Watch your depth and take care not to exceed the maximum depth for the gas mix you are using. Oxygen poisoning gives no warning before it strikes. If there is no one immediately available to help you if you have an oxygen seizure you will almost certainly die. If at any time you suspect something isn't right shift to your bail-out system and abort the dive.

Be sure to check the pressure gauge for your bail-out bottle occasionally while you are underwater to make sure the system has not developed any leaks.

Be sure to check your bail-out bottle occasionally during the dive to ensure that you are not losing gas pressure through any leakage. You never want to find yourself in a situation where you need your bail-out bottle and suddenly discover that it is empty. Without your bail-out bottle you will be unable to inflate your buoyancy compensator and will have no gas to make a normal ascent or precautionary decompression stop. In a borderline no-decompression situation this could lead to decompression sickness.

Making "yo-yo" dives where you make multiple ascents and descents during a single dive is never a wise idea. If you use a rebreather this type of dive profile will cause you to waste breathing gas. Every time you ascend with your rebreather you lose the gas in the breathing bag. If you descend again, the bag must fill for your new depth. Make another ascent and you lose that gas. Avoid this type of dive profile whenever you dive, but especially if you are using a rebreather.

NORMAL ASCENTS

Prior to any direct ascent to the surface you want to take a few moments to pause on the bottom and make sure you are ready to come up. Locate your power inflator for your buoyancy compensator and be ready to vent air if you added gas to it during the dive. If you are wearing a dry suit make sure that your exhaust valve is open so you are prepared to vent gas as you come up.

With a semi-closed circuit system it is critical that you purge the breathing system before starting your ascent. This will help ensure that you have the maximum ppO_2 in the breathing bag as you come up. If you were working hard immediately prior to your ascent the ppO_2 in the breathing bag will be quite low. If you then fail to purge the system, as you rise through the water column the surrounding pressure decreases, and the ppO$_2$ in the bag will fall even further. If it gets low enough you could pass out during the ascent due to hypoxia. This can be fatal.

You will also find that as you ascend, the gas in the breathing system will expand as the surrounding pressure decreases. When this happens the excess gas will vent out through the exhaust valve. However, you will usually find, depending upon the back-pressure setting of your exhaust valve, that your buoyancy will increase as the gas expands in the breathing bags. Be prepared to vent gas from your buoyancy compensator or dry suit to counteract the increased buoyancy in the breathing bags. It is recommended that your first few ascents with a rebreather be made next to a weighted line until you become accustomed to the changes in buoyancy that you will experience with the unit upon ascent.

Some divers also find that as the gas expands in the breathing bags upon ascent they have a more difficult time exhaling into the rebreather. If this situation affects you, it is

perfectly acceptable to exhale through your nose rather than into the rebreather as you ascend. You won't be wasting any gas because this volume would be lost during the ascent anyway. You can also open your exhaust valve slightly to accomplish the same thing.

Be sure to make a precautionary decompression stop (safety stop) at the end of every dive.

Be sure to make a precautionary decompression stop (safety stop) at the end of your dive to help avoid the possibility of decompression sickness. Just because you are breathing nitrox doesn't mean that you can't get bent. Don't forget to purge your breathing bag one more time before you do your final ascent from your precautionary decompression stop.

EMERGENCY PROCEDURES

Probably the most common "emergency" situation that you might face at some time during your rebreather adventures is having your mouthpiece knocked out of your mouth due to a careless buddy or your own clumsiness. When this happens, your mouthpiece will float over your head with nitrox bubbling vigorously out of it. No water can enter the mouthpiece or rebreather as long as the gas is flowing strongly out of it. It is important to recover the mouthpiece as quickly as you can to avoid losing a large quantity of breathing gas.

You must be able to recover the mouthpiece on your rebreather quickly.

To recover the mouthpiece you will need to tilt your head back and lean slightly backwards from the vertical position to get the mouthpiece and hoses at the proper angle to recover them. Grab the mouthpiece and pull it down to your mouth, keeping your head tilted back. As long as you do this quickly, little or no water will enter the rebreather and you should be able to resume your dive without a problem.

If you have been properly trained for rebreather diving, adhere to your training, and set up and maintain your equipment correctly, it is unlikely that you will ever have a failure of your rebreather while you are underwater. However, like all mechanical things, rebreathers can fail and you need to understand what to do in the event of an emergency.

You must be able to recognize the signs of a rebreather failure, some of which are very obvious while others are quite subtle. Early recognition of a failure can mean the difference between life and death.

In virtually every case of a rebreather failure your response to the emergency will be the same; i.e., go on bail-out. Be sure to close the lever on the rebreather mouthpiece before you remove it from your mouth. Once you are on your bail-out system you must make an immediate ascent to your precautionary decompression stop depth, complete the stop, and ascend to the surface. Once you have switched to bail-out you must not continue to dive unless you are needed to make an immediate rescue of another diver. This is the only situation that would justify delaying your ascent.

Close the lever on the rebreather mouthpiece before you remove it from your mouth. This must be an automatic habit.

You must always be prepared to switch to your bail-out system in the event of an emergency.

FLOODED SCRUBBER CANISTER

In the event your canister floods, it will usually become obvious that there is a problem very quickly. Several different clues will alert you to this problem including a loss of buoyancy, an increase in breathing resistance, and an unusually large amount of gas being lost through the rebreather's exhaust valve with each exhalation. These are all reliable signs that you have a serious problem. You can also expect that you will get a build-up of carbon dioxide in the system, and there is the risk of chemical burns as well if you do not switch to your bail-out quickly.

Baffle systems and improved absorbents in today's rebreathers make "caustic cocktails" less likely a phenomenon than they were in the past. However, accidents can and do still occur.

Flooded scrubbers are usually the result of either failing to close the lever on the mouthpiece during a surface swim, poor maintenance of your system, or incorrect assembly. Always check your rebreather over carefully prior to assembly and again once it has been put together.

If your system has flooded it will need to be disassembled and cleaned immediately following the dive. In most cases, fresh water will be all that is needed to rinse the system, but check your owner's manual in case there are any special instructions for your rebreather.

CO_2 ABSORBENT AND SCRUBBER FAILURE

The carbon dioxide absorbent used in your rebreather can fail under a variety of circumstances. Absorbent that is stored improperly, with the lid off or loose, will react with the carbon dioxide found in air and lose its effectiveness.

Under no circumstances should you use the absorbent in your scrubber for any time longer than the recommended duration of the scrubber canister. Absorbent can lose its capacity for carbon dioxide removal quite rapidly, exposing you to a dangerous level of CO_2.

As mentioned previously, your scrubber can also fail if it is not fully packed properly, leading to channeling of exhaust gas through the scrubber with no reaction. Always shake your canister prior to loading it into your rebreather and listen for loose absorbent. Add more absorbent if the canister is not tightly packed.

During your dive you should always be monitoring your-self for any change in your breathing pattern that would indi-cate a build-up of carbon dioxide in your system. In any situa-tion where you expect scrubber or absorbent failure you should immediately switch to your bail-out and proceed to your precautionary decompression stop.

BREATHING BAG OR HOSE FAILURE

In the event that your breathing bags or hoses fail, your system will not breathe properly, leak gas, and begin to fill with water. These changes in the performance of your system should become obvious fairly quickly. Don't delay in switch-ing over to your bail-out system and starting your ascent.

OXYGEN SENSOR FAILURE

Although the reliability of underwater electronics has increased tremendously over the past ten years, there is always the possibility that your oxygen monitoring system can fail during a dive. With a mechanically controlled semi-closed circuit rebreather it is possible to dive without the benefit of the electronics to monitor the oxygen in the system, but unless you have been trained to dive this way, it is not recommended.

If your rebreather is electronically equipped and the electronics fail you should switch over to your bail-out and start your ascent.

POST DIVE PROCEDURES

Once you have ascended from your dive, swim back to the boat or beach using your rebreather. Get in the habit of keeping the mouthpiece in your mouth until you are back aboard the boat and have turned the gas cylinder off. Remember, never leave a semi-closed circuit rebreather on if you are not diving, unless you intentionally want to empty the cylinder.

If you have sufficient gas left in your cylinder, and time on the absorbent in your scrubber, you may want to make another dive without changing cylinders or refilling the scrubber. This is perfectly acceptable and is done by rebreather divers all the time, provided the dive is made the same day. However, if you will not be diving again until the next day or later, the rebreather should be disassembled, cleaned, and properly stored until you plan to go diving again.

If you plan to make another dive the same day, it's a good idea to open up the shroud and check your breathing bags to ensure that they do not have an excessive amount of moisture in them. A small amount of moisture is normal, due to saliva entering the breathing hose, leakage around the mouthpiece, and water liberated by the absorbent chemical process. Unless

Between dives, check your breathing bags to ensure they do not have an excess of moisture inside them.

there is more than a few tablespoons worth of water in your rebreather you should not be concerned.

Be sure to allow yourself the minimum 90 minute surface interval to allow the CNS level of oxygen in your body to drop prior to making your next dive. Remember that most training agencies recommend no more than three nitrox dives during a single day of diving.

If at all possible, store your rebreather out of the sun during the trip home. Corrugated breathing hoses are susceptible to damage from the sun's rays.

MAINTENANCE AND STORAGE

Follow the directions in the owner's manual for cleaning and maintaining your system. Rebreathers require more maintenance than open circuit equipment and that maintenance must be done promptly.

After diving, a rebreather should be disassembled down to its component parts and thoroughly cleaned. It is extremely important to flush the breathing hoses, bags, and scrubber with plenty of fresh, clean water.

*Be sure to rinse all of the
components of your
rebreather thoroughly, per the
manufacturer's directions.*

If your manufacturer recommends the use of a disinfectant be sure to use it only as directed. Breathing bags and corrugated breathing hoses are great places to grow bacteria if they are not properly cleaned and dried. Using a disinfectant becomes more important if you are responsible for a rebreather that will be used by multiple divers in rapid succession and the rebreather has no chance to completely dry out.

Rebreather components should be dried in a location where there is plenty of air circulation, but out of direct sunlight. Some divers build special drying cabinets for their rebreathers with forced air circulation to ensure proper drying. Corrugated hoses need to be hung up to dry so that any water inside them can drain out rather than remain trapped in the corrugations.

Breathing bags will usually need to be drained more than once over the course of several days after diving to eliminate any water than pools inside them. The baffle systems used in modern rebreathers (to prevent water from entering the scrubber) makes it difficult to get all of the water out of the breathing bags after they have been rinsed.

Your rebreather should be stored in a cool, dry place, away from electric motors and hot water heaters. These devices produce ozone which attacks rubber parts.

On most rebreathers the lever on the mouthpiece should be left in the open position during storage. However, you should follow the storage procedures recommended by the manufacturer of your system.

CHAPTER 6

FULLY CLOSED CIRCUIT ELECTRONIC REBREATHERS

> ## WARNING:
>
> This chapter contains procedures for diving fully closed circuit mixed gas rebreathers. These procedures are for general information only, since each model of rebreather has its own specific procedures. While the principles of operation will be the same or similar for each system, use only the procedures you have been taught for your specific rebreather.

THE NEXT STEP IN REBREATHER EVOLUTION

Fully closed circuit mixed gas rebreathers are the next step in the evolution of rebreathers. They are the most sophisticated type of rebreather and are generally more expensive and complex than semi-closed circuit systems.

A fully closed circuit mixed gas rebreather (hereafter referred to as a "CCR" or "rig") is the most versatile kind of rebreather because, unlike oxygen rigs or semi-closed systems, time and depth are much less of an issue. Due to their ability to be extremely efficient with a small gas supply, offering bottom times from three to ten hours at nearly any depth (dependent on brand, configuration and water temperature), these systems give the diving professional an edge no other system can match.

Many professional underwater photographers have turned to fully closed circuit rebreathers not only because of a CCR's ability to safely extend their time with a subject, but also because a fully closed system bubbles only during ascent, making working with skittish animals a little easier. However, if you think you will become invisible to sea life, you won't. The animals can still see you and may choose to react to your presence by swimming off. Yet, you will find that the lack of bubbles and regulator noise will more often allow for a closer approach to certain creatures.

Deep wreck divers as well as technical and cave divers have used CCRs to allow them to shed the large number of tanks they must carry when diving open circuit. Recognizing a closed circuit rebreather is easy. If you see a diver with what looks like a very complicated Hoover vacuum cleaner on his back, it is probably a CCR.

There is a popular myth about fully closed circuit rebreathers, which is that you must be a rocket scientist to dive with one. That is not exactly true. Granted they are more complicated than open circuit and more sophisticated than semi-closed, however, once you understand partial pressures, the rest is just plumbing and batteries. It is also useful to realize that all your previous open circuit experience is just about worthless for diving with a CCR. Much of what you know about buoyancy control, monitoring your air supply, decompression limits and emergency procedures must be relearned for diving a CCR. These systems are so different you will probably find that after strapping on a closed circuit rig, using one is like learning to dive all over again.

In making the decision to buy a CCR, a good question to ask yourself is, "Am I very comfortable about which end of a

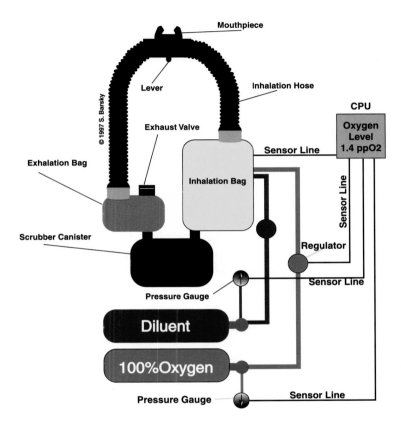

Fully closed circuit electronic rebreathers are more complex than semi-closed circuit systems. This schematic shows the layout of a "typical" closed circuit rebreather

screwdriver to use?" Unlike any other piece of equipment that can be returned to a local dive shop for service, you will become more intimate with your CCR than anyone else will. You will be responsible for preparing your life-support system for a dive, for post dive maintenance, general upkeep, periodic disinfecting and keeping a detailed logbook. Yes, you must maintain a log. You must be comfortable working with electronics, tubing, batteries, oxygen sensors and in some cases, even computers. If you're not, or if you're not meticulous about pre-dive prep and maintenance, you won't live too long diving with a fully closed circuit rebreather.

You must maintain a logbook regarding the maintenance and repairs you have performed on your rebreather to help ensure your safety.

HOW CCRS WORK

A CCR is essentially a "nitrox-mixing machine on your back." It can provide you with the optimum mix of oxygen and nitrogen (or heliox, or trimix) regardless of your depth. The biggest difference between semi-closed systems and fully closed is the way they deal with the partial pressure of oxygen.

The partial pressure of oxygen (ppO_2) is the most important concept to understand before using a CCR, because it is the key principle in how a CCR operates. Controlling the partial pressure of oxygen is what makes diving a CCR work. Since changes in depth affect the partial pressure of oxygen, and you have complete control over your gas mixture, you must understand the consequences of any action you take and how it can help or hurt you.

When you dive with open circuit nitrox or semi-closed rebreathers, you always have depth limitations. This happens because you are diving with a fixed percentage of oxygen in your bottle. The partial pressure of oxygen (ppO_2) increases with your descent, until you reach your safe limit (1.6 maximum) and decreases with your ascent. This is not very efficient from a decompression standpoint, because a higher ppO_2 is more beneficial at shallower depths.

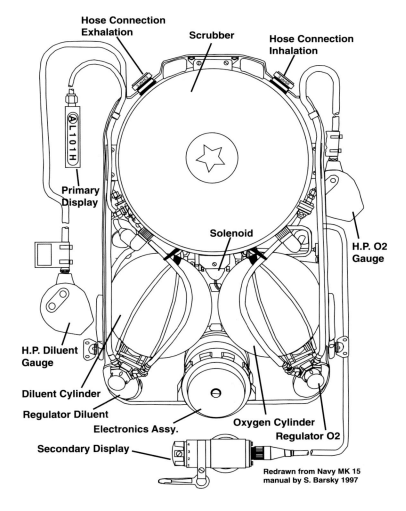

Bio-Marine's rebreathers are electronically controlled but do not use a microprocessor.

A CCR on the other hand can maintain a set ppO_2 by changing the percentage of oxygen in the system, decreasing the percentage as you descend and increasing it as you ascend. A closed circuit rebreather is able to lower the percentage of oxygen during descent by automatically, or manually, adding a diluent (pronounced as "dill-you-ent") gas. Usually that gas is air, however deeper divers may choose heliox or trimix.

Because a CCR has the ability to sense ppO_2 it will automatically (or manually if required) add oxygen to the breathing loop as it detects a dropping ppO_2 either from normal respiration or from ascending. It is common for CCR divers to maintain a partial pressure of oxygen between .7 and 1.3. By maintaining a high ppO_2 the CCR diver is able to benefit from longer no-deco times and more efficient decompression.

Some rebreather designs, such as the Bio-Marine CCR155 and the newer BMR500 use electronics to control the oxygen level in the system, but the electronics are not dependent on a microprocessor. Many divers favor these designs for their simplicity and their lack of dependence on system software.

Newer rebreathers, like the CIS-Lunar, the Prism Topaz, and Undersea Technologies systems use microprocessors to control the oxygen level in the breathing loop. This will allow you to download extensive information about your dive and your rebreather's behavior during the dive.

COMPONENT SYSTEMS OF CCRS

There are three major sub-systems common in all CCRs. Like semi-closed circuit systems, a CCR will include a breathing loop, pneumatics, and electronics. Some of these components will be almost identical to those found in a semi-closed circuit system, while others will be very different.

The breathing loop contains the counter lung (or breathing bags), carbon dioxide scrubber, and the breathing hose assembly, just like you would have in a semi-closed circuit system. However, the CCR will also have oxygen sensors in the breathing loop. A semi-closed circuit rig can have sensors too, although their purpose will generally be strictly to help

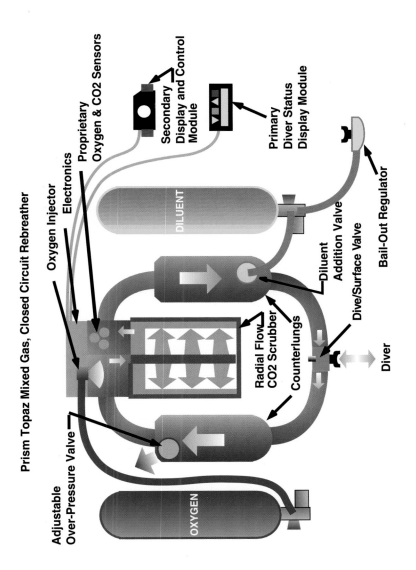

This schematic of a Prism Topaz system illustrates the breathing loop, pneumatics, and electronics

monitor the oxygen level in the system rather than to control it.

The pneumatics assembly consists of two or more cylinders of breathing gas, high pressure regulators to lower the pressure of each, bypass valves that allow for manual addition of those gases and a diluent addition valve inside the breathing loop. This valve automatically adds diluent gas as the diver descends to compensate for the increasing depth compressing the breathing loop volume. One cylinder contains pure oxygen, the other a diluent gas containing air or in certain circumstances, heliox or trimix. A pressure gauge for each gas supply is also used. Again, most of these components would all be similar to those found in a semi-closed circuit system.

The electronics and battery assembly are the brains of the fully closed circuit electronic rebreather. The electronics take the information from the oxygen sensors and control the addition of oxygen into the breathing loop by a solenoid valve. This system is the main difference between most semi-closed circuit systems and fully closed circuit systems. The electronics assembly includes a set of displays that show the status of the rebreather and the partial pressure of oxygen in the breathing loop. These are called the primary and secondary displays.

Typically the primary display is analogous to the "idiot lights" in your car. The primary can let you know that everything is "OK" with your system, or it can alert you to a problem by giving you an alert light. If you see an unexpected indication on your primary display, it is telling you to check your secondary display.

Secondary displays show the partial pressure of oxygen measured by each sensor. Using that information allows the CCR diver to troubleshoot any gas problem that may arise and take action. More sophisticated secondary displays may also show decompression status and tank pressures.

You should also know that typically the secondary is separate from and redundant to the primary display. What this means is that even in the event of a battery or electronics failure, the secondary will still operate. This can allow you to control your rebreather manually.

INSIDE THE BREATHING LOOP

When you exhale into your rebreather, one-way valves in your mouthpiece insure that the flow goes only in one direction. That exhaled breath first passes through your exhalation hose to the scrubber where carbon dioxide is chemically removed. Next, the gas flows over three or more oxygen sensors.

You can think of an oxygen sensor as simply a battery, or fuel cell, that operates in the presence of oxygen. The sensor itself consumes a very small quantity of O_2 and gives off a voltage in direct relation to the partial pressure of oxygen in the loop. The greater the partial pressure of oxygen, the greater the voltage. If the partial pressure drops, the voltage drops as well.

The voltage released by the sensor is detected by the electronics and measured. If that voltage is higher than, or equal to, the partial pressure setpoint you wish to maintain, the electronics does nothing. If the voltage drops, corresponding to a drop in ppO_2 due to your use of the oxygen in the loop or during ascent, the electronics causes a solenoid valve to open, which injects a measured dose of O_2 into the loop. This process repeats itself until the partial pressure returns to the set point. While all of this takes place automatically, in the event of a battery or electronics failure, it can all be controlled manually by using the oxygen by-pass valve.

During descent, diluent gas is automatically added to the breathing loop to maintain volume so you can take a full breath and to prevent the partial pressure of oxygen from getting too high. There is a manual by-pass so if needed, diluent can also be added manually.

During ascent, the ppO_2 decreases with the dropping ambient pressure, so oxygen will be injected to maintain your setpoint. Also, the volume in your loop will expand and need to be vented into the water. All CCRs have a dump valve that actuates as the loop volume expands, and you also have a back-up valve built in. Your personal exhaust valve is your nose. That's right, if necessary you can vent through your nose (this assumes you are not wearing a full-face mask where your nose and mouth are in the same compartment).

One of the major advantages of fully closed circuit rebreathers, compared to semi-closed circuit systems, is that they maintain a constant partial pressure of oxygen, regardless of depth.

ADVANTAGES OF FULLY CLOSED CIRCUIT ELECTRONIC REBREATHERS

Fully closed circuit rebreathers offer many advantages over semi-closed circuit rebreathers, for divers who can use their capabilities. These advantages include:

- CCRs are capable of longer dives than semi-closed systems
- CCRs maximize your bottom time by constantly providing the best gas mix regardless of depth.
- CCRs minimize your inert gas absorption.
- CCRs provide very efficient decompression.
- Closed circuit rebreathers look very cool.

Because a fully closed circuit rebreather does not vent your breathing gas except during ascents, a small supply of breathing gas can go a long way. Your diluent supply is only used during descent to provide you with the volume to breathe. Once you have reached your diving depth, the only gas you consume will be your oxygen supply.

Quite often you will find that your diluent gas will be almost full even at the end of hours underwater. Typically, the greatest advantage of a CCR is the ability to make very long dives whether for work or pleasure. You might think that this efficient use of gas would also allow for many shorter dives to be done without refilling your bottles. Technically, this is true. However, since the amount of gas you carry is generally much less than you would when diving any other way, it is always wiser to start all your dives with full bottles.

Note in the table on page 150, how a CCR maintaining a set ppO2 of 1.3 changes the percentage of oxygen with depth. You can see how this benefits your no-decompression limits as well.

You can see that on a dive to 60 feet you would have 46 percent oxygen in your rebreather. With that percentage of oxygen, the equivalent air depth is 31 feet. Giving you a no-decompression time of 200 minutes! Ascend to 40 feet and the rig would automatically increase the O2 percentage to 58. The increasing oxygen percentage during ascent is beneficial because it increases the rate at which your body off-gasses absorbed nitrogen or any other inert gas you use.

The upshot of all this is that by constantly optimizing your gas mix you can increase your no-decompression limits and make mandatory decompression safer and more efficient. A CCR also is capable of allowing you to make your shallow stops on nearly 100 percent oxygen.

Note that at a depth of 170 feet the percentage of oxygen is 21, the same as air. This is called a "crossover point". To maintain a partial pressure of 1.3, past 170 feet, the CCR will lower the percentage of O2 to less than 21 percent. What this means to the diver is that at this point you are breathing a gas mix that has more nitrogen (greater than 79%) than air.

Depth	Oxygen Percentage	Equivalent Air Depth	No-Decompression Limit, U.S. Navy
10	100		No theoretical limit
20	80		No theoretical limit
30	68		No theoretical limit
40	58	6	No theoretical limit
50	51	18	No theoretical limit
60	46	31	200
70	41	44	100
80	38	56	60
90	34	70	50
100	32	81	30
110	30	94	25
120	28	106	20
130	26	119	15
140	24	133	10
150	23	145	5
160	22	157	5
170	21	170	5
180	20	183	Not recommended
190	19	196	Not recommended
200	18	209	Not recommended

Table 6.1 Partial Pressure of Oxygen Maintained at 1.3 (No-decompression limits from U.S. Navy tables)

Continue deeper and you can see that the equivalent air depth actually increases due to the extra nitrogen in the mixture. The effects of nitrogen narcosis will also increase with an increased percentage of nitrogen. At this point, it is better to dive with a diluent gas other than air. The crossover point varies with the partial pressure setpoint. At a ppO_2 setpoint of 1.0 for instance, the crossover is 125 feet. At a lower setpoint of .7, (this is where most military rebreathers are set) the crossover point is only 77 feet. You can see how the higher your ppO_2 setpoint, the deeper you can go before hitting the crossover point.

During the decompression phase of the dive, you can enhance your nitrogen elimination by raising the ppO_2 in your CCR to close to 100% at decompression stops shallower than 25 feet. Of course, you must be extremely careful not to return to depth with a high ppO_2 in your rig.

REBREATHERS LOOK COOL!

Okay, so maybe this is not really a benefit, but still, it is an impressive sight to see someone diving a closed circuit rebreather. Watching someone moving quietly through the water with no bubbles is definitely weird when you first see it.

DISADVANTAGES OF FULLY CLOSED CIRCUIT REBREATHERS

There are many disadvantages to using a fully closed circuit rebreather, and for some divers, these drawbacks may be greater than the advantages. Aside from the physical hazards of using a fully closed circuit rebreather (see Chapter 4), there are other distinct liabilities that are incurred when you select this type of dive gear.

- CCRs are the most expensive type of self-contained diving gear available.
- CCRs require more training than semi-closed circuit rebreathers.

- Traveling with a CCR requires more planning and equipment, and will probably be more expensive if you travel outside the U.S.
- Pure oxygen is not always readily available and is hazardous when handled improperly.
- Although it may be advantageous not to produce any bubbles when you want to get close to certain types of marine life, sometimes the absence of bubbles can put you in danger.

You need many tools and spare parts to keep a closed circuit rebreather operational.

CCRS ARE EXPENSIVE

A fully closed circuit mixed gas rebreather ranges in price from $6,500.00 to $20,000.00, and that is just the beginning. Training, spare parts, oxygen and carbon dioxide absorbent are all additional expenses that you must budget for to support a CCR. Okay, so now you have a fancy new rebreather that will allow you to spend five straight hours underwater. Is the rest of your equipment, including your dive computer and thermal protection, up to the task?

A diver using a CCR will need to have various spare parts including the following:

- Hoses, up to $90.00 per hose. You need two, and you should have two as spares. Some rigs have 4 breathing hoses.

- Oxygen sensors. You need three at $100.00 or more each. They last anywhere between six months to a year, and the smart diver always has several extra as spares.
- Batteries. Their duration is dependent on the type of CCR, but spares are a must.
- Carbon dioxide absorbent. Absorbent costs $80.00 to 160.00 per five-gallon pail. The amount of time you get out of a container will vary between CCRs, however, around 30 hours of dive time per 34 lbs. of absorbent would be a good estimate.
- Spare mouthpieces, bottles, solenoids, switches, O-rings, O_2 grease, tools and more are all needed to insure an operable CCR.

Spare hoses can get quite expensive. This diver is wearing a UT240 rebreather.

TRAINING

At present there are only a few people actively involved in training others to dive these rigs. Typically you will invest about 40 hours of your time and up to $5000.00 of your money for training. If there is no training in your area you may have travel expenses as well.

In most cases, advanced nitrox training is considered a prerequisite for rebreather diving. Your rebreather training should stress the manual operation of your system, trouble shooting, and emergency procedures.

Knowing how to handle the manual operation of your particular CCR is a must. Typically, most instructors will not allow you to even turn the electronics on in your rig until the end of class. Diving a fully functioning rebreather is very easy. Flying your rig without electronic control is a real confidence builder because you will develop your skills should you ever have an electronics failure. Manual operation will also improve your understanding of partial pressures by requiring you to control your rebreather throughout your training.

You must be trained to handle every possible emergency that may occur when you use a CCR, from simple problems like recovering your hoses to dealing with complete system failure.

Understanding the mechanics of your rig is necessary in spotting potential problems before you dive. It is here where developing the self-discipline to follow a checklist and maintain a logbook can make your CCR diving reliable and enjoyable. Learning the correct pre and post dive procedures will save you time and trouble later.

Perhaps the most important aspect of closed circuit rebreather diving is the emergency procedures, or "E.P.s" for short. This is where you learn to cope with problems in your rig. What do you do when a sensor dies? What happens if the battery or electronics fail? Can you continue to dive? What can you do if you lose your oxygen? One CCR instructor calls these "boom scenarios". You are diving along when all of a sudden "BOOM!", something breaks. Now, what do you do?

Your training should emphasize the practice of these E.P.s under controlled conditions to the point where your reaction to a problem is automatic.

Diving a CCR can be comfortable and enjoyable provided you take the time to get properly trained.

TRAVEL

If you want to take your rig on a dive trip, be prepared for extra baggage fees when you show up with 70 lbs. of rebreather, tools, an extra case or two for spares and a couple of buckets of CO_2 absorbent at the airport. You may find that by removing the scrubber and the bottles, then packing them in a separate container, you can save on overweight charges.

Make sure you bring along a Material Safety Data Sheet (MSDS) with your absorbent for the airline to see. These documents can be obtained from your CO_2 absorbent supplier. An MSDS will tell the airlines that you are not trying to bring a harmful chemical on board. Trying to fly with full diluent and oxygen cylinders is a federal no-no. Drain your gas cylinders before you get to the airport.

Your rebreather should be packed in a rigid container with plenty of foam padding to prevent shock and damage to your rig. It is a good idea to protect the displays in the same way. Remember, you are traveling with an expensive piece of gear that while rugged, is likely to be handled by gorillas.

Other questions that need to be answered before you travel include:

- Does the dive operation or boat allow a rebreather?
- Is there space aboard the boat to accommodate your rebreather, consumables, and spares?
- Is there CO_2 absorbent available locally?
- Is a supply of oxygen readily available?

The logistics of traveling with a rebreather must be planned in advance.

OXYGEN LOGISTICS AND SAFETY

Owning your own rebreather will require you to handle oxygen. To do that you must be prepared to use the correct techniques, o-rings (viton) and lubricants (such as LTI's Christolube) to manage oxygen safely.

To fill your oxygen bottles, look for dive shops that fill nitrox. They will usually have oxygen available. If your local dive shop doesn't have it you'll have to rent your own bottle from a gas supplier. This can run $5.00 to $10.00 per month and around $40.00 to refill a large bottle.

There are three grades of oxygen available: aviators, medical and industrial oxygen. Aviation and medical are the same purity, however, aviation grade is moisture free to prevent icing at high altitude. Industrial grade used for welding is breathable, but can have objectionable odors, so this grade is not desirable for use in CCRs.

If you plan on traveling with your rebreather, make sure you find out if O_2 is available. In some places, a doctor's prescription is required to obtain medical oxygen.

NO BUBBLES, SOME TROUBLE

Despite their advantages, there are times when diving a CCR can be a little troublesome and require you to be more alert. Unlike open-circuit, or even semi-closed circuit, it is nearly impossible for someone to track you underwater. You must be very aware of any activity around you.

On at least two separate occasions dive boats have dropped anchors near divers on CCRs. These boat captains did what every responsible boat driver would do. They slowly approached the dive site, noted where the open circuit divers were by their bubbles, then, moved off to drop their anchors. Unfortunately, they had no way of knowing there were divers with closed circuit rebreathers on the bottom within inches of where their anchors landed. This is a mistake they would not have normally made had they seen air bubbles. Luckily, the CCR divers were alert and heard the noise of the boat and the anchor chain on its way down.

Another near-miss incident occurred with a CCR diver doing a safety stop on an anchor line. On the surface the boat skipper saw a panicked scuba diver and rapidly pulled up the anchor line to make a rescue. The anchor came up so fast that one of the flukes snagged a breathing hose almost pulling it off the rig of the CCR diver. The CCR diver was able to react quickly enough to prevent an accident, but the boat skipper had no idea what happened until he returned later to pick up his other divers after they had surfaced.

To help prevent accidents like these, it's essential to inform the boat captain or divemaster of your intended dive profile and direction. Often times, dive boat operators will have a time schedule they want to keep that may not coincide with your ability to spend hours underwater. It is considered polite to let the skipper know how long you would like to be down and in what general direction you plan to go. Many boat captains are a little nervous about rebreathers if they have no experience with them, so be responsible to help ensure that rebreathers will be welcome in the future.

Not all dive boat skippers are familiar with the capabilities of closed circuit rebreathers.

RIGGING YOUR SYSTEM

Rigging a closed-circuit rebreather for a dive is largely a matter of hose and cable management. With two or four breathing hoses, two pressure gauges, an open-circuit regulator with a low pressure hose, a bail-out bottle, BC hoses, drysuit hose, straps, buckles, a primary display and a secondary display each with its own cables, even a loaded tech diver looks streamlined by comparison with a rebreather diver. So what can a CCR diver do to keep from looking like a swimming hairball?

Some of the best things you can add to your system are the new underwater retractors. These are spring-loaded reels like the school janitor wore for his keys. Mounted on your harness, they work very well to keep displays close to your body and out of the way. Pull out your instruments to view them, release and the display moves back to its original position. Velcro straps, bungee cord or latex tubing are all helpful in reducing CCR clutter. Proper management of all your dangling hoses, gauges, and displays is a safety issue, too.

Keeping all those hoses and cables under control can prevent entanglement or possible damage to your rig. Even with these precautions, you should always be aware of where everything is both above and below the water. Coral, shipwrecks, rocks, cleats and boat ladders can all snag the unwary.

Use retractors to control the displays and gauges that make up your system.

Rebreathers made by Rexnord or Bio-Marine (CCR 155 and BMR 500) typically have a basic harness with no BC. These units come with the same type of harness the military uses. It is up to the diver to either use a horse collar BC or make modifications to the unit to allow for another type of BC or harness to be attached.

Some of the first divers to use these systems have made many modifications to make their style of diving easier. For example, deep wreck divers have adapted a "wings" type buoyancy compensator system that allows for the placement of extra gas supply bottles. Others have adapted weight integrated buoyancy compensators to replace the original harness. Each group has made changes to their systems to enhance the type of diving they do. Rebreathers from companies like Steam Machines and CIS-Lunar Development are normally supplied with back mounted buoyancy compensators.

If your rebreather was not delivered with a buoyancy compensator you will need to mount one on it.

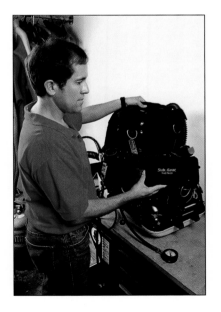

BAIL-OUT BOTTLES

The need for a bail-out bottle varies with the kind of diving you are doing and the type of CCR you own. Some rebreathers have the capability of using your onboard diluent supply (usually air) as open circuit bail-out. Since this is generally less than 30 cubic feet of gas, you should decide if the amount of gas you carry is sufficient to get you safely to the surface based on your expected dive profile.

Obviously, if your dive will have mandatory decompression, or if you are using trimix, heliox or cave diving you will need to plan for a proper amount of gas to be readily available should the need arise. In this case, a separate bail-out system is usually essential.

Some divers have made modifications to their systems to allow the on-board oxygen to be used in the open circuit mode at shallow depths. If this is done, it is imperative that you have some way of locking that switch so you cannot accidentally breath pure O_2 below 25 feet.

If your rig has access to your diluent for open circuit bail-out, an isolation valve between your second stage and hose is a good idea. Made by Zeagle Systems, the isolation valve allows you to shut off the flow of air to your second stage in case of free flow. This can help prevent the catastrophic loss of gas.

An isolation valve between the first and second stage of your bail-out regulator is a good idea if you use your diluent for open circuit bail-out.

PRE-DIVE PREPARATION

Regardless of the type of CCR you buy, there will be a pre-dive "prep." You must follow this procedure to insure an operable rig underwater. The following pre-dive prep is fairly "typical" of what needs to be done to prepare a rebreather to dive.

While different CCRs are similar in many ways and the pre-dive set-up will also be similar, the procedures for your rig may not be exactly what we have outlined here. This is only an example of what you need to do prior to diving with a "typical rebreather."

We've presented this example so you can get some idea of the number of steps involved in setting up a CCR. While none of these steps are difficult, there are many more of them than the few steps involved in setting up open circuit scuba.

Use a checklist to ensure that you are following the correct procedure for the set-up of your rebreather.

> **WARNING:**
> Be sure to follow the exact procedures you learned during your training for preparing your specific model of rebreather for diving. Use a checklist to ensure you are following the correct procedure and no steps are left out.

- Inspect for dirt, deterioration and damage during each pre-dive step.

  Replace any parts that are not functioning correctly or show heavy wear.

- Test the operation of the one-way valves in the mouthpiece.

  With the hoses disconnected from the rebreather, open the mouthpiece valve. Next breathe from the mouthpiece insuring that your inhalation and exhalation enters and exits from the correct hose. To check the exhalation valve, inhale while closing off the inhalation hose end. You should not be able to inhale at all. If you can, you have a leak in the exhale valve. To check the inhalation valve, exhale while closing off the exhalation hose end. If you can feel leakage, there is a problem in your inhalation valve.

• Fill scrubber canister.

Be sure to wear gloves and eye protection to avoid getting absorbent dust on your skin or in your eyes. After correctly packing your scrubber, always use the shake test prior to installing it in your rig. Hold your scrubber up to your ear and shake. If it rattles, the absorbent has settled or there wasn't enough to start with, so refill it until you hear no rattles!

Be sure to test the operation of the one-way valves in the mouthpiece.

Fill the scrubber canister carefully.

• Check/replace moisture absorbers.

Foam absorbers are used in some rebreathers to soak up excess moisture to avoid wetting out the CO_2 absorbent. They may also serve as a spacer to fill the uneven space between the absorbent and the top of the can-

ister. They should be dry before they are installed in your rebreather.
• Check O_2 sensor wires.

These wires must be intact to get a proper reading at your displays.
• Take sensor readings in air.

Most CCRs use a triple redundant system, i.e., with three oxygen sensors. The sensors must all be working properly. Any sensor that does not read properly must be replaced.

Ideally, the best method is to test your sensors under pressure, and some rebreathers such as the Prism Topaz will allow you to do this. If your CCR is not capable of having its sensor housing pressurized, you should then check your sensors with 100% oxygen to make sure they are reading a ppO_2 of at least .95.

Oxygen sensors must be tested before each use.

• Re-install canister, ensure o-rings in good condition.
• Inspect and check mouthpiece and breathing hoses.

There must be no cracks or punctures in the hoses. Replace the hoses if they show any signs of damage.
• Check the battery with a multimeter.

The battery should have more than sufficient power for the dive that you have planned. The battery normally will power the primary display and control the flow of diluent and oxygen into the breathing loop. If the battery fails underwater you can still operate the rebreather manually.

The battery must have more than sufficient power for the dive that you have planned.

- Install battery and battery housing cover, then tighten bleed screw.

- Install O2 and diluent bottles.
   These bottles should always be full at the start of any dive.

- Open diluent shut-off valve.
   This is the valve on the diluent cylinder.

- Test operation of diluent bypass valve.
   The bypass valve allows you to add diluent manually should the electronics fail.

You should always have more than enough gas to complete your dive.

• Bottom diaphragm to test diluent addition valve.

This is done by inhaling through the mouthpiece to suck all the gas out of the system. When you have inhaled all the gas, the diluent addition valve should add gas to the system if it is working correctly.

• Open O_2 valve.

This is the valve on the oxygen cylinder.

• Test operation of O_2 bypass valve.

The oxygen bypass valve allows you to add oxygen manually should the electronics fail.

• Turn on the electronics.

The rig should adjust the oxygen level correctly for sea level. You should be able to hear the valve operating as the system adds oxygen.

• Check the sensor readings with the secondary display.

All three sensors must be reading properly.

• Check for leaks by totally submerging rig, ensure mouthpiece remains in closed position.

All three sensors must be reading properly.

By submerging your pressurized rig in a tub of water, you will quickly see if there are any areas where your limited gas supply is leaking from the system. Make any repairs prior to diving, then do another leak test.

If for some reason you are unable to do a submerged leak test, there is another way. Turn on both bottles. Then with your mouthpiece valve closed, fill your loop with oxygen until you hear the exhaust valve burp. Then wait and watch. The loop volume should not change. If it slowly deflates, there is a leak. If the exhaust valve burps again, you have a leak somewhere in your pneumatics system. Next, turn off both bottles, tap both bypass buttons to bleed off a little pressure and look at both pressure gauges. The pressure in both should remain steady. If the pressure increases, you may have a valve problem or just did not turn it off completely. If the pressure decreases, you have a leak somewhere in either the diluent or oxygen side. You can tell which side is leaking by which gauge shows the drop in pressure. In any case, make repairs before diving.

• **Turn power switch off until you are ready to dive.**

If it seems that there are a lot of steps you must go through to dive a CCR, you are right. This list does not include the calibration procedure, which you must do prior to any series of dives. The calibration procedure is used to ensure that your sensors and electronics are functional. That procedure will be different for each brand of rebreather.

You must always test your rebreather for leaks before the start of your dive day.

You may have heard the term "flying a rig" when it comes to diving a rebreather. This is really not far from the truth. Just as a pilot has to preflight his aircraft, the CCR diver must pre-dive his rig. For both, it would be a serious lack of judgment not to perform all of the required inspections and tests.

Like the pilot, a rebreather diver must keep an eye on his instruments to "fly" safely. Unlike aircraft, however, the CCR diver is usually in much better condition after a scrubber "crash" than a pilot. The bottom line in diving a CCR is to take your time and do your pre-dive preparation right.

It's easy for a new rebreather diver to get too cocky after a few successful dives. Diving a rebreather is easy, and once you have a number of dives under your belt, the worst thing you can do is get complacent. Pre-dive preparation should be followed before any series of dives, and a double check of your rig between dives is smart.

GAS SELECTION AND ANALYSIS

Unlike semi-closed systems where a premixed nitrox blend is the only gas supply, diving a CCR is a little simpler in that you need not decide what mix to use prior to diving. The closed circuit rebreather automatically mixes the diluent and oxygen for your depth and gives you a read-out of its ppO_2.

Analyzing your gas prior to a dive is typically not necessary for a CCR diver unless you are using a mixed gas like trimix or heliox. In general, for dives to 170 feet, air is used as the diluent gas and reliable sources can be found worldwide. Oxygen, as discussed before, can be harder to get, but standards for medical grade oxygen are very high and reliable as well.

If you are traveling out of the country, especially to any third world nation, having an oxygen analyzer to double check the quality of the O_2 you get is a good idea. You may also need to bring the appropriate fittings to fill your oxygen bottle. Different countries have different standards for their oxygen connections, so research that before you leave.

PLANNING A DIVE

To plan a rebreather dive, there are three things you must know; 1) your ppO_2 setpoint, 2) the maximum depth you plan to dive to (in atmospheres), and 3) the percentage of oxygen based on factors 1 and 2. From these three pieces of information you can effectively plan your dive time around the dive tables.

For example, let's say that you are planning a dive to 60 feet. You need to convert 60 feet into atmospheres (ata.) which is 2.8 ata. You decide that the setpoint on your rig will be 1.3 ppO_2. By dividing 2.8 by 1.3, you will get the fraction of oxygen (percentage) at 60 feet which is .46 or 46%.

By knowing what the percentage of O_2 is at your maximum depth, you can now figure what your decompression limits are by using the equivalent air depth (EAD) formula. The EAD for a 60 foot dive with 46% oxygen is 31 feet. The no-decompression limit for this dive is 310 minutes (according to the U.S. Navy tables).

An alternative is to use a nitrox computer programmed with the percentage of oxygen that reflects the deepest point of your dive. Whether you use this method with a table or nitrox computer, it will be inherently conservative because it does not take into account that the percentage of oxygen increases as you ascend.

You can use a nitrox comput-er programmed with the per-centage of oxygen that corre-sponds to the deepest point of your planned dive.

Several rebreather man-ufacturers offer dive com-puters specifically design-ed to track your ppO2 and provide you with deco information. This kind of system will give you the greatest flexibility and the longest no-decompression times because it can take into account the increasing O2 per-centage as you ascend during a multi-level dive.

A word of caution, any type of "saw tooth" dive profile (i.e., multiple ascents and descents) is not only a bad idea in general, it is especially bad while using a rebreather. Doing many ascents and descents during a dive is very wasteful of gas. Go up and the expanding gas vents out. Go back down and more gas is added to the loop. Use your common sense and this will not be an issue.

If you plan to make a decompression dive you should fol-low the rule of thirds used by cave and wreck divers, i.e., allow one third of your gas for the descent, one third of your gas for the ascent, and keep one third reserved for emergen-cies. Thus, if your rig has a six hour capability, your bottom time should not exceed two hours to maintain an effective margin of safety.

DONNING A CCR

Putting on your fully closed circuit rebreather is much like putting on a set of doubles. It will probably be heavy, perhaps a little cumbersome and have an abundance of hoses, cables and displays hanging around.

Extra care should be given to your primary and secondary displays when preparing for a dive. They should be placed somewhere where they will not get damaged or crushed accidentally. Be sure you have your displays hooked where they belong before getting up and moving around. They will almost always swing wildly at the end of their cables and hit the nearest hard object. If they were to hit something soft, like your buddy, it would not be so bad, at least for you! However, your buddy may get upset about getting whacked by a gauge in the face. Of course, it will definitely ruin your day if you break a display.

Your buddy should understand your rebreather system.

Depending on the design of your rig, you may need to have a buddy pass you your breathing hoses. Just prior to your dive, do a buddy check. Verify that each of your rebreathers is ready to dive.

Double check the following items just before you get in the water:

- Your diluent and oxygen bottles are both on.
- The ppO2 is where you want it to be set in your loop.
- Your hoses, cables and displays are routed cleanly and safely.
- The latches (if applicable) on your shroud (or cover) are closed and locked.
- Your breathing hoses must be secure.

At this point, turn your rig on and check your displays. If everything is working, exhale, put your mouthpiece in, open the valve and go for a long dive.

ENTERING THE WATER

You can enter the water in any fashion you would with open circuit. However if you have a long drop off a boat, it is easier on you and your rig to go down the boarding ladder. Remember, keep all your hoses and cables under control to avoid snagging them during entry.

IN THE WATER

Once you and your buddy have entered the water, allow a little time to pass so any trapped air in the cover can bubble out. Then take a good look at your buddy's rig to make sure there isn't a stream of bubbles coming out of the rebreather. Although it is easier to have your partner visually check your rig, you can also do it yourself. Rolling onto your back and watching for a bubble stream is one method, or carrying a small mirror is another.

If you make a rapid descent, starting with a high ppO2, you may find that the fast increase in pressure will cause a temporary "spike" in your ppO2 well over your setpoint. This spike can be dealt with in several ways. If the increased ppO2 is not objectionably high, you can do nothing. You will simply metabolize the oxygen in your loop and it will settle down to your setpoint. If the ppO2 is too high, add diluent to reduce it.

With practice and experience, another way to manage this spike is to learn where starting ppO2s end up at depth. For example, by starting your dive with a ppO2 lower than 1.0, you will discover that by the time you reach your target depth, your ppO2 will reach your setpoint and not go over it. This technique does take time, observation and practice.

One mistake beginning CCR divers often make is to periodically exhale through their nose. While certainly an okay practice when diving open circuit, it is very wasteful of gas on closed circuit. You will want to have the best fitting mask possible as well. Clearing your mask on occasion is fine, but if your mask leaks a lot, it is time for a new one.

It should also be routine for you and your dive buddy to keep an eye out for leaks during a dive. If you have a minor leak and you are not losing gas at a rate that will affect your safety, you can probably continue to dive. However, if you are making a decompression dive, or you have a major leak, you need to get out of the water and correct the problem.

During the dive it is important to monitor your primary display on a regular basis. Your secondary display need not be monitored as frequently, but should be checked to confirm that your primary is providing the proper information.

If your system is functioning properly you should not need to touch the bypass controls or cylinder valves during the dive. However, if you should have a component failure, you will need to control your system manually. See the section later in this same chapter on emergency procedures.

As the warm moist gas travels through your breathing hoses, condensation will eventually form and collect by your mouthpiece. In addition, after an extended time underwater, you can have quite a bit of saliva in your mouthpiece. This can be a small problem if you are not prepared for it.

If you have been drooling in your mouthpiece and happen to look up, don't be surprised if you get a shot of water and saliva back into your mouth. If you are unprepared, you might inhale some of this and choke a little. You can often hear the water gurgle a little by the one-way valves in your mouthpiece as you inhale or exhale.

Monitor your primary display on a regular basis.

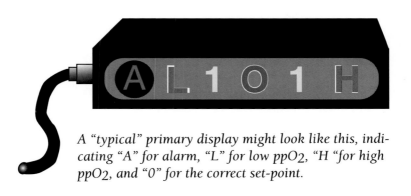

A "typical" primary display might look like this, indicating "A" for alarm, "L" for low ppO2, "H "for high ppO2, and "0" for the correct set-point.

There are several things that you can do to remove that water. By rotating your head so that the exhalation hose points down, blow forcefully to drive it back into the loop. This technique is similar to clearing an old double hose regulator. Some mouthpieces have the ability to purge any water by closing the valve and venting it into the water. The other method is to just tip your head back and drink it. After all it is just distilled water that has come from you and the scrubber reaction. Obviously, you must use your judgment and common sense before doing this. You never want to confuse normal condensation with the possibility of a "caustic cocktail".

BUOYANCY CONTROL

One of the first things you will discover when diving a CCR is how easy it is to remain neutrally buoyant. Since you don't exhale into the water, your buoyancy does not change as much during a dive as with open circuit.

For those of us who are used to exhaling to submerge, you will find that with a CCR, nothing happens, you will still float. You must swim to change your altitude in the water or add a little extra weight. Since your exhaled breath just goes around in circles, you will typically have to deal with the excess buoyancy this creates. This will involve the placement of weights near the counter lung to offset its lift.

An easy test to see if your buoyancy is correct is to dive your rig and lay face down on the bottom of a pool, relaxed. Is it easy to maintain your position or does the rig feel like it is lifting your torso off the bottom? If it is, you may find some experimentation with counter weights helpful. Over a long dive, too much lift can cause strain to your lower back from fighting to stay level.

EMERGENCY PROCEDURES

Since fully closed circuit rebreathers have more components than semi-closed circuit systems there is more potential for the failure of an individual system component. You must have the experience and training to deal with each of the emergencies described below to be a successful (i.e., living) rebreather diver.

FAILURE TO TURN THE REBREATHER ON

It's a simple but deadly mistake to leave your rig turned off when starting a dive. During descent, diluent gas would be added, so you would have the volume to breathe. You would eventually use the oxygen in your loop and find yourself breathing a hypoxic mix. Preventing this situation is very simple. Make sure you follow your pre-dive checklist and more importantly, check your displays. The primary display will not be on if the power is off and the secondary will show your ppO_2 regardless.

FAILURE TO TURN THE OXYGEN SUPPLY ON/RUNNING OUT OF OXYGEN

Leaving the valve on your oxygen bottle off will cause hypoxia if you aren't alert to your displays. This is the same situation as above. The solution would be to check your secondary and O_2 pressure gauge regularly, then turn on your oxygen valve.

There are also a couple of ways to run out of O_2. One is to have done a very long dive without checking your O_2 pressure gauge. Another would be to have an o-ring or burst disk failure. Your options are to fall back on an appropriate bailout, or use your CCR in a semi-closed fashion. Diving your CCR in a semi-closed fashion is covered later in this chapter.

LOSS OF DILUENT

Of all the problems you can have underwater with a rebreather, losing your diluent is one of the easiest to solve. Typically, you might hear a "POP" and the sound of gas blowing into the water. Quickly shut both tank valves and check your pressure gauges. Whether it's because of a blown o-ring, ruptured high pressure hose, or failed burst disk, all your diluent is lost.

Since diluent is only used as you descend to maintain your loop volume, this is generally not a big deal. Simply abort your dive and ascend. The rig will vent and add oxygen as you ascend.

You may need to shut off your diluent if your system develops a leak.

SOLENOID FAILURE

The solenoid valve that controls oxygen addition usually fails in the closed position. Once again, the best solution is to always know just what your ppO2 is by checking your secondary display often. Oxygen can then be added manually. In some rebreathers the operation of the solenoid creates an audible click and hiss every time the rig adds O2. Remember, the CCR adds oxygen in relation to your work rate.

The harder you work, the more often your rig will add oxygen to make up for what you have metabolized. After you have some time on a CCR you will develop a sense of how often the solenoid will activate by what you are doing. Work hard and you will hear the sound of O2 injection more often. If you rest on the bottom, you will hear it less. Once you become accustomed to hearing that, not hearing that periodic noise serves as a warning.

If the solenoid were to fail in the open position, you would hear oxygen hissing into your loop followed by a change in buoyancy and/or the exhaust valve dumping the gas into the water. Well-designed rebreathers have an orifice that limits the free flow of oxygen if such an event occurs. Again, turn off the rig and open or close the oxygen supply valve as necessary to maintain the proper ppO2.

Be aware that in some rebreathers the oxygen addition can be very quiet. On this type of rig you may be able to feel a slight increase in volume in the breathing loop when O2 is added.

You can manually add oxygen by opening the bypass valve. The diver's thumb is on the by-pass valve.

BATTERY FAILURE

If the battery were to fail on a dive, the solenoid would stop functioning and your primary display would be off. Maintaining a good dive log that tracks the number of hours your battery has been in operation and knowing the manufacturer's battery life expectancy will help to eliminate this problem. However, batteries can and do fail before they are supposed to, so once again, regularly check your secondary. You can then add O2 manually while monitoring your ppO2 with your secondary display.

During ascent the partial pressure of oxygen drops. Fix any problem first, keep an eye on your displays, then ascend and add oxygen manually as required using your bypass valve.

Fortunately, unless you are working very hard, changes in your ppO2 occur fairly slowly. Regular checks of your displays make hypoxia unlikely for the well-trained diver. The truth is that the easiest way to "go hypoxic" is to ignore your maintenance, your rebreather log and most importantly, your displays.

SENSOR FAILURE

On older rebreathers like the MK 15 and CCR 155, a sensor failure causes a drop in the total voltage the electronics reads. The drop in voltage makes the electronics assume the loop ppO$_2$ is low when it is not. This lights the alarm light on the primary display and causes the solenoid to fire once every five seconds.

Part of diving a rebreather involves not only looking at your displays, but listening as well. If you have missed looking at your primary display, your hearing can tell you something is amiss by the number of times oxygen gets injected into your system. The solution on one of those rigs is to turn off your electronic control and go to manual.

Quite often the alert CCR diver can stop this problem before the ppO$_2$ climbs too high. However, if after checking your secondary display you find your ppO$_2$ unacceptably high, flush the loop with diluent to lower the ppO$_2$. Newer rebreathers have more sophisticated controls that disregard a bad sensor. The electronics will alert you to its failure, but the rebreather will remain functional.

COMPUTER OR ELECTRONICS FAILURE

If either were to fail and instruct the solenoid to fire continually, high ppO$_2$ is the likely result. How high it gets is dependent on how alert and observant you are. Remember, look and listen. The correct action is the same as if your sensor fails, i.e., switch to manual control and ascend if your dive is not of a critical nature.

MANUAL BY-PASS BUTTON STICKS OPEN

This one will be pretty obvious since you will hear as well as feel the jammed button. Turn off the oxygen cylinder valve. Use the valve to manually add O$_2$ when it is needed.

ABSORBENT FAILURE/CO_2 BUILDUP

It should be noted that the symptoms of excess carbon dioxide are not always reliable before they may cause you to pass out, and they share similarities with hypoxia and CNS oxygen toxicity. This is another reason why paying attention to your displays and maintaining a log is so important.

Many CCR divers who have experienced hypercapnia have reported air hunger, headaches and fatigue as typical, with the symptoms subsiding if they stop swimming or ascend. This makes sense, because a diver at rest produces less CO_2 than a swimming diver and ascent will cause the partial pressure of the carbon dioxide to drop.

It has also been reported that on one occasion a diver noticed fatigue symptoms in his partner and correctly guessed his buddy's scrubber had crashed, before the buddy realized it. Obviously, this kind of observation comes with time, experience and knowing each other's abilities.

If your scrubber fails, switch to open circuit bail-out and ascend immediately.

If you find that you are experiencing symptoms of hypercapnia, abort your dive. Switch to open circuit bail-out and immediately start your ascent. This is the first and most obvious choice.

In the event your bail-out system is not functioning properly, a less desirable option is to stop all exertion, ascend to lower the partial pressure of carbon dioxide and purge your loop to remove the excess carbon dioxide, then add fresh O_2 and diluent. You may find that this combination can allow you to make an ascent to the surface should another form of bail-out be unavailable.

A failure of the one way valves in the mouthpiece can also cause CO_2 poisoning. These valves are similar to the exhaust valve in an open circuit second stage. It is possible to have one fail or stick open. In a regulator, you will know this because it will flood and repairing it is as easy as removing the exhaust tee. In a CCR mouthpiece, unless you check the operation of those valves prior to diving, use of a failed valve will allow you to re-breathe your CO_2 rich exhaled breath.

CAUSTIC COCKTAILS

Following the required maintenance and pre-dive inspection of your breathing hoses can make the chance of this problem extremely unlikely. Most rigs are very capable of tolerating small amounts of water that can enter by accident. However, should you hear a significant amount of gurgling and feel resistance to breathing indicating water in your loop, you should abort your dive, turn off your mouthpiece and switch to open circuit bail-out.

Remember that loss of your loop volume will cause you to be negatively buoyant. You must be prepared to take corrective action if this occurs.

If absolutely necessary, some rebreathers, such as the Cis-Lunar, allow for a flooded scrubber to be purged and reused, allowing you to use the rig long enough to surface. However, in most cases, the safest course of action in any scrubber flood (or suspected flood) is to shift to your bail-out system and abort the dive. Even if it is possible to de-water the CCR underwater you would not want to rely on the absorbent to perform at its full capacity or function properly.

If you discover a small leak and you manage to stop it you will still have doubts as to whether enough water entered the system to affect its operation. If you inhale water and soda lime you could start an uncontrollable cough that may not even make it possible to breathe from a regulator on open circuit.

Each manufacturer has emergency procedures that deal with how to handle a flooded rebreather. Most of these procedures are system specific.

The most likely causes of a flooded system are:

- loose hose fittings
- old damaged hoses
- old damaged mouthpieces
- bad o-ring seals
- damaged purge valves

Again, all of these problems are preventable in your pre-dive prep.

Another possible problem is the dust from CO_2 absorbent. If you are not careful when filling your scrubber, dust from the CO_2 absorbent can be inhaled. A few steps to reduce that possibility have already been discussed, however, they bear repeating.

- Let a slight breeze blow off some of the dust as you fill your canister.
- Don't use the last inch or so of material in the bucket, because that is where most of the dust has settled.
- Always wipe off your scrubber before installing it to remove any dust that accumulated during filling.

ASCENDING AT THE END OF YOUR DIVE

Ascending at the end of your rebreather dive is done the same way as any other type of dive, i.e, ascend slowly.

You will notice several things happening with your rig as you ascend. First, keep an eye on your secondary display. You will note that as you rise and the ambient pressure drops, so will your ppO2. The dropping ppO2 will cause your rig to almost continually add oxygen.

Some rebreathers get more buoyant as you ascend. Be prepared to vent your dry suit or BCD, if needed.

As you ascend and the pressure drops the gas in your breathing loop will expand. Obviously, this gas must vent out of the system or it would damage your rebreather. You may find that as the gas expands, it can be a little more difficult to exhale. This happens because as the volume of gas in your loop expands, the loop will fill and you will be exhaling against the vent valve spring. If you find this uncomfortable, feel free to vent some gas from your nose.

Some rebreathers may get noticeably buoyant as you ascend. Be prepared to vent your drysuit, BCD, or if needed, vent your rig through your nose. This will allow you to control your ascent.

PRECAUTIONARY DECOMPRESSION STOPS OR ACTUAL DECOMPRESSION

One of the big advantages to closed circuit rebreathers is the ability to raise the oxygen level in the system for your precautionary decompression stop or actual decompression obligation.

One of the advantages of a fully closed circuit rebreather is the ability to do shallow stops (20 feet or less) on pure oxygen. This will provide you with an enormous safety factor whether used during a precautionary decompression stop or actual decompression.

To raise the level of oxygen in your system you will need to purge the breathing loop a few times by exhaling through your nose and adding pure oxygen. Remember, this should only be done at 20 feet or shallower.

Even though you have purged the system you will not be able to completely eliminate all nitrogen from your rebreather as nitrogen "washes" out of your body in response to the high percentage of oxygen in the breathing loop.

SEMI-CLOSED CIRCUIT OPERATION

Diving your rebreather in a semi-closed mode is possible and is done by exhaling every third or fourth breath into the water through your nose. This technique is considered an emergency procedure only and is not to be used for routine dives. You may need to do this technique for two reasons:

- You have had your scrubber crash and do not have a bail-out.
- You have lost your oxygen supply and do not have a bail-out.

In the first case it is assumed that you have a fully functioning rig with the exception of the scrubber. The carbon dioxide level has risen to the point where you feel symptoms of hypercapnia. After purging the loop and adding fresh gas to reduce the level of CO_2 (see hypercapnia), you ascend which lowers the pp CO_2. If you feel it necessary, you can exhale every third or fourth breath into the water to further reduce CO_2 levels.

The second possibility is that you have lost your oxygen supply. This is the classic "BOOM" scenario. After hearing a lot of gas escaping into the water, you shut both tank valves and check both pressure gauges to determine which gas you are losing. Somehow, an O-ring, HP hose or burst disk on your O_2 bottle has failed and all you have left is diluent which you turn back on.

Keeping an eye on your secondary display, exhale every fourth breath into the water, then flush your loop with diluent for 5 seconds. Obviously, diving this way you would expect your ppO_2 to drop, and it will. Try to keep your exertion level to a minimum and keep close track of your ppO_2. If you need to increase your work level, you may need to exhale every third breath.

Each of these techniques should be included in your training and should be practiced until you are comfortable. If you are diving with a Prism Topaz this has a built-in semi-closed circuit capability that you should be able to use.

POST DIVE MAINTENANCE

Careful maintenance of your rebreather is one of the keys to safety in rebreather diving. You must be religious in your attention to your rebreather at the end of each diving day.

After dive maintenance will take you about 30 to 40 minutes longer than the time you would spend maintaining open circuit gear. That's assuming that you are exceedingly thorough when you clean your system. In any case, plan on spending around an hour and a half to two hours total for post dive clean-up. Aside from the normal things you would do in cleaning any dive gear, a rebreather has some special considerations.

Be sure to carefully rinse your rebreather at the end of each diving day. Soaking the system in fresh water is preferred.

• It is a good idea to soak your rig in a large container of fresh water. This will accomplish two things. First, it will remove any saltwater from the rig. Secondly, it gives you another opportunity to leak test your system. With the gas system on, take a good look at the rig's plumbing. Any leaks or problems should be repaired before you store your rebreather.

• Oxygen sensors should be dried and stored in an airtight container. Keeping O_2 sensors in a small airtight container may prolong their life span by temporarily putting them to "sleep." The sensors will slowly use up all the oxygen in the container, leaving them packed in nitrogen. Removing them for use will reactivate them. Use a desiccant pack or silica gel like that used to store photo gear to ensure they are in a dry environment. With some rebreathers, the oxygen sensors are not easily removed, so always follow the manufacturer's recommendations for storage.

• After every day of diving, the breathing loop should be rinsed with fresh water and allowed to dry. Rinsing your hoses between dives is also a good idea. Drying the inside of your hoses or breathing loop can be difficult. Some divers have made blowers or drying cabinets for this purpose.

Lysol IC Quaternary cleaner is a strong disinfectant. It must be properly diluted before use.

• Periodic disinfection of your hoses and the breathing loop is a good idea and essential if more than one person is using the rebreather. The corrugations of the breathing hoses make a great breeding ground for bacteria and fungus if they have not been properly rinsed and are allowed to stay damp. The breathing bags are also another site where nasty "bugs" can grow.

There are several commonly accepted solutions that can be used to clean your loop. Betadine is a common liquid disinfecting agent that can be effectively used in a dilute solution, but can leave an objectionable odor and taste.

Lysol IC Quaternary cleaner is a concentrated liquid that is mixed with water. It is mixed in the proportion of one half ounce to a gallon of water. Use only the disinfectants that are recommended by the manufacturer of your rebreather. Make certain you rinse your loop and hoses with plenty of fresh water after using any of these products. Common sense should dictate how often you disinfect your system.

Rinse the hoses thoroughly after each day of diving.

Of particular importance to the CCR diver is the scrubber. Proper logging of dive times, correctly packing your scrubber and replacing the CO_2 absorbent at the correct intervals recommended by the manufacturer of your rig is critical. Failure to do so will lead to a scrubber "crash" and hypercapnia.

Each manufacturer will have a recommended scrubber duration that should always be followed. That duration will be listed in hours or minutes and it is here that keeping a detailed log is so important. After each dive, you should write down the length of your dive and add that to the past dives you've made, keeping a running total on the number of hours on your scrubber. For example, let's say your scrubber has a duration of five hours. You have been diving all day and have put 3.5 hours on your scrubber. If your next dive is going to be 1.5 hours or longer, very strenuous or in cold water, it is time to replace the CO_2 absorbent. A good rule of thumb is "absorbent is cheap, when in doubt, throw it out."

CHAPTER 7

REBREATHER DIVING ACCESSORIES

You can make your rebreather diving safer and more enjoyable through a number of additional items such as full face masks, dive computers, oxygen analyzers, and disinfectants. As with any dive equipment, proper training is required to use specialized items such as full face masks and dive computers, even though these items are relatively simple to use.

FULL FACE MASKS

A full face mask can be an important safety addition to your rebreather. By wearing a full face mask you reduce the risk of drowning should you pass out underwater. Of course, if you are unconscious and not breathing you could still die, but the risk of water inhalation and the prospect of drowning is greatly reduced.

One of the side benefits of wearing a full face mask is that it also provides you with the ability to talk since you are not clenching a mouthpiece between your teeth. At short distances, under five feet, you can communicate without the need for any electronics. At greater distances, the addition of an electronic wireless system will allow you to communicate freely under a wide range of conditions.

Another advantage to using a full face mask is that it can give added protection in biologically polluted water by keeping water away from your eyes, nose, and mouth. This is a real consideration for search and rescue divers who must dive in harbors, irrigation canals, and other similar locations.

Many full face masks are sold with a built-in second stage, which isn't usable with a rebreather. You will only be able to use a mask that is designed to accept a variety of mouthpieces.

In selecting a full face mask your primary consideration must be whether or not the opening for the mouthpiece is compatible with your rebreather's mouthpiece mounting tube. If the full face mask will not seal over the mouthpiece mounting tube securely it must not be used with your rebreather.

Before you dive with a full face mask you must be trained to use it properly.

Your second consideration in choosing a full face mask must be the fit of the mask, including not only whether it seals properly on your face, but whether or not it's comfortable to wear. Getting a proper seal can be difficult for divers with thin or small faces. The comfort of the mask is largely dependent on the material used to make it, but is also affected by the design of the straps, any equalizing devices, and its buoyancy.

In evaluating a full face mask for use with your rebreather, consider the following features, too:

- Lens: The lens should be made of either tempered safety glass, Lexan® or a similar impact resistant plastic with excellent optical qualities. In addition, the mask must have good visibility.
- Frame: The mask should have sufficient rigidity so that it stays in one position on your face. The frame must also provide support for the lens.
- Mask straps: The straps allow you to adjust the tightness of the mask. When you're wearing gloves, it's easier to handle large, rugged straps than it is to adjust thin, flexible straps.
- Equalizing device: The mask should have some provision for grabbing or blocking your nose to help you to equalize the pressure in your ears.
- Oral/nasal mask: Some masks will include a separate chamber for either your nose and mouth, or just your mouth, to help cut down the "dead air space" inside the mask. This helps to reduce the amount of carbon dioxide in the mask. Without a separate breathing chamber, the first gas that you inhale will be the gas you just exhaled.
- Low volume: Ideally, you want as low a volume in the mask as possible. This will help eliminate jaw strain from a buoyant mask lifting upwards on your jaw.

If you have the opportunity to try the mask underwater with your rebreather before you buy it, be sure to take the time to do so. A mask that feels comfortable in the dive shop when you have it on for a few moments may be very uncomfortable after you have worn it for 90 minutes underwater.

When you dive with the mask to evaluate its fit and comfort be sure to wear any hood that you might normally wear for diving to see how the mask fits with your hood. Some hoods may need to be trimmed to work with certain full face masks.

If you plan to use wireless communications with your rebreather you should also test the particular model of wireless you plan to buy with the specific full face mask you want to use to ensure that it works satisfactorily. Some masks provide higher intelligibility than others. Certain wireless systems perform better than others.

Make sure any wireless system you plan to use is compatible with the full face mask you select. The unit on this mask is made by Ocean Technology Systems.

One of the problems with most full face masks is that once you put the mask on your face, you are committed to using your breathing gas supply. If you have to stand around on the deck while you wait to get in the water, you can end up using quite a bit of your gas. In addition, once the mask is on, your intelligibility to other people who are standing by on the deck is very limited.

If you are using a conventional full face mask with your rebreather and have a long surface swim at the end of your dive, or if you have used up your gas supply you will need to remove the full face mask in order to breathe. This can be a distinct disadvantage in choppy seas if you do not have a scuba mask or snorkel.

Another drawback with most full face masks is that if the mask floods due to a broken lens or other failure while you are underwater, not only will you not be able to see but you will not be able to breathe. As a rebreather diver you must also decide how you will deal with a rebreather failure underwater if you are using a full face mask. In order to access your bail-out supply, in most cases you must remove the full face mask to use your open circuit regulator. This situation will leave you "blind" underwater unless you have had the foresight to carry a scuba mask with you to use if this situation occurs.

Probably the most versatile full face mask to use with a rebreather is the M-15 full face mask designed by Morgan Diving Corporation of Santa Barbara, California. The mask is unique in that it has an upper chamber that covers the eyes and nose, like a conventional scuba mask, and a detachable lower chamber or "mouth pod" that only covers the mouth. The lower pod can be easily installed or removed both topside and underwater.

The M-15 mask can be worn on deck without the mouth pod in place until you are ready to enter the water. This allows you to talk on the surface. When you are ready to dive the mouth pod snaps into place and you open the lever on your rebreather. (Note: with a pure oxygen rebreather there is a special purge procedure you must follow prior to diving.) You can keep the mouthpiece in your mouth or you can just breathe into the mouth pod.

The biggest advantage of the M-15 underwater is that it allows you to remove the mouth pod without removing the entire mask. This makes it easy to switch over to your bail-out in the event of an emergency, yet still allows you to see. You can even use a snorkel with this mask for surface swimming if the need arises.

One other advantage to a full face mask is that many divers find that it is easier to equalize their ears underwater when they don't have to grip a mouthpiece with their teeth. Divers who normally need to block their nose and exhale to equalize often find that with the regulator out of their mouths they can clear by merely yawning or wiggling their jaw.

The Morgan M-15 mask is unique in that it provides a lower chamber for your mouth and an upper chamber for your nose and eyes.

Like any piece of specialized equipment, you must be trained to use a full face mask if you have never used this type of gear before. Although this equipment is not complex, proper procedures must be learned.

One of the most serious concerns when you use a full face mask is learning to deal with a flooded mask. With a conventional full face mask, that covers the eyes, nose, and mouth in one chamber, clearing the mask while on open circuit scuba is not much of a problem, since the purge button on the second stage can be used to flush the mask. When you use a rebreather, however, clearing a conventional full face mask is a bit of a problem since there is no purge button on the rebreather mouthpiece. This is not a problem with the Morgan mask, since your nose and eyes are in a separate chamber from your mouth.

With some back mounted rebreather systems you may be able to clear the mask by rolling on your back so that the breathing bags are below the mask, which should cause the system to free flow. With other systems you may find that you need to use your bail-out to get a good enough breath to clear the mask. Of course, if the mask is dislodged from your face it is essential to close the lever on the mouthpiece quickly to avoid flooding the rebreather.

If your rebreather does flood and you have the mask on, another danger with conventional full face masks is that not only will your mouth potentially be exposed to caustic chemicals, but your nose and eyes will, too. With the separation of your nose and eyes from your mouth that occurs if you dive with the Morgan mask, there is little if any chance that your nose and eyes will be exposed to a caustic mix in the event of a rebreather system flood.

With the Morgan M-15 full face mask it isn't necessary to remove the whole mask to use your bail-out system.

DIVE COMPUTERS

The ideal dive computer for your rebreather is integrated with the breathing loop of your system, continually senses your ppO2, and can be adjusted for the particular mixed gas that you are using. As more rebreathers become available for the recreational diver, you can expect to see more and more dive computers with this capability.

If you are using a nitrox gas mixture, there are many different dive computers on the market that will provide satisfactory decompression information for you. It's wise to take the conservative approach to planning your dives, and use the air diving no-decompression limits as the basis for your bottom time. If you follow this procedure, you will have a wide safety margin in the event that something goes wrong and you must overstay your planned bottom time. If you conduct your nitrox dives according to the air diving tables, you can use your existing dive computer that was designed for air diving.

For semi-closed circuit systems with a single gas cylinder, an integrated hoseless dive computer is recommended, but should be used in conjunction with the submersible pressure gauge supplied with the system. This gives you a level of redundancy in monitoring your gas supply in the event that either the computer or the gauge fails. The integrated computer will also give you your projected remaining bottom time based upon your present gas consumption rate. This is another feature that can be helpful in conducting your dive.

A back-up dive computer is considered a wise investment, especially if you are diving on a multi-day trip with your rebreather. Without a back-up computer you will be out of the water for a day if your sole computer goes down.

If you are doing decompression dives with your computer, a back-up computer is considered absolutely essential. Without a back-up computer, if you have a lengthy decompression obligation and your primary computer fails, you will almost certainly suffer from a serious case of decompression sickness. Always carry a back-up dive computer if you are doing decompression diving.

Marco Flagg of Desert Star Systems was the first to design and build integrated dive computers for rebreathers that would sense the ppO2 and make the appropriate decompression calculations. He has also designed underwater tracking systems and developed an underwater GPS (Global Positioning System) receiver. The system shown here was an early prototype.

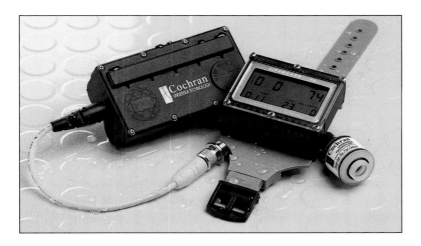

Cochran's Lifeguard computer takes readings from an oxygen sensor, monitors, ppO2, and computes your decompression.

OXYGEN ANALYZERS

If you are involved with any type of diving where you are using gas mixtures other than air, an oxygen analyzer is a necessity. Even if you analyze your breathing gas at the dive store where you have your cylinders filled you will probably find it essential to have an analyzer available for your personal use. It's much more convenient to be able to analyze your gas at home if you misplace a cylinder tag and are uncertain what gas mixture is in a particular cylinder than to return to the dive store to check what percentage of oxygen is in your tank. In addition, when you do the pre-dive checks for your system you'll need to be able to double check the gas you are using.

Oxygen analyzers are electronic instruments that use what's known as a "fuel cell" to detect the percentage of oxygen, up to 100%, in any given mixture. The fuel cell is generally not visible in the analyzer but is covered by a protective screen. Both the analyzer and the fuel cell are delicate items and will not withstand much abuse, so care must be taken in handling them. As you might expect, both items are also expensive.

Oxygen analyzers also use batteries, but they draw very little power from them. If your analyzer begins to give questionable readings try replacing the battery first, although in most cases a fuel cell failure is more likely.

Fuel cells periodically need to be replaced; they do not last forever. Certain types of fuel cells can fail in less than a few months. You can also ruin a fuel cell by dropping it or pushing in on the membrane where the gas mixture flows across the cell.

If the fuel cell begins to fail you will probably find that you cannot calibrate your analyzer properly, or the analyzer "drifts" and the reading keeps changing. If you notice either of these things happening, or you cannot get a reading from the analyzer at all, it's a safe bet that the fuel cell has either begun to fail or has failed completely. Replace the cell before analyzing any diving gas.

The electrolyte found in fuel cells is caustic. If you find that your fuel cell is leaking, use a pair of rubber gloves to remove it, carefully wipe up the interior of your analyzer, and dispose of the cell.

If you are using your analyzer at altitude you must take into account the change in atmospheric pressure. See the manual that came with your analyzer for the correct procedure for using your particular unit at extreme elevations.

To analyze compressed gas properly, you must use a device that restricts the flow of gas across the fuel cell surface. Most analyzers sold for recreational/technical diving are sold with a restrictor that connects to a standard low pressure inflator, such as those used for buoyancy compensators.

Your oxygen analyzer can be calibrated on air or with pure oxygen.

To use your analyzer, remove the protective cap from the sensor, turn the analyzer on and wait at least five minutes for the readings to stabilize. Calibrate the analyzer, either with room air or 100% oxygen. Connect the restrictor to your gas cylinder, turn the gas on, and connect the fitting to the analyzer. Wait at least one minute for the analyzer to stabilize before recording the reading.

When you have finished using the analyzer be sure to turn it off and cap the sensor opening. Store the analyzer in a cool, dry location.

CHAPTER 8

IS THERE A REBREATHER IN YOUR FUTURE

Now that you've read this far you probably have a pretty good idea of whether or not a rebreather is the right piece of dive gear for you. Rebreathers certainly aren't for everyone. They require discipline, knowledge, experience, practice, and maintenance. The following quiz should help you decide whether a rebreather is the right piece of equipment for your type of diving.

- **Do you have a specific need or application for a rebreather?**

If you are a serious underwater photographer a rebreather may make a lot of sense for you. Similarly, if you are a small boat owner, a rebreather can save you a lot of deck space and allow you to take extended dive trips without the need for a compressor. However, if you typically make only one short dive a day, in shallow water, there isn't much point in owning a rebreather.

- **Do you have a good understanding of nitrox and/or mixed gas diving procedures?**

You must have a thorough understanding of partial pressures and the problems involved any time you dive with mixtures other than air. Without this understanding, you will not be able to use your rebreather with any degree of safety.

Rebreathers make sense for divers who have specific applications for them.

• **Do you have the money for the initial purchase and continued operation and maintenance of a rebreather?**

Rebreathers are expensive and maintaining a rebreather is also expensive. There are more components that must be replaced to maintain a rebreather on an annual basis. In addition, the cost of consumable items is higher than for open circuit air diving.

• **Do you have the time to devote to pre-dive preparation and post dive maintenance?**

Setting up a rebreather takes more time than setting up open circuit scuba. Post-dive maintenance takes more time, too. You cannot be casual about setting up and maintaining your rebreather. It helps to be a borderline obsessive/compulsive to be a safe rebreather diver...

- **Do you have the mechanical aptitude to perform the required pre-dive prep and post dive maintenance?**

If you aren't comfortable handling tools then you won't enjoy working on a rebreather.

- **Do you have a good understanding of the theory and practice of rebreather diving?**

You can't just buy a rebreather and go diving. You must get the training you need for the specific model of rebreather you intend to use. If you switch rebreather models, you will need new training for this different equipment.

- **Do you have the diving expertise to rig your rebreather in a way that is comfortable and enjoyable to use?**

Everyone's diving is a bit different and you must rig your rebreather so that it works best for you. Your system may require longer or shorter hoses to work with specific accessories. You may need to clip your gauges in particular positions to make them accessible.

Purchasing a rebreather is a personal decision that only you can make. You must have the right aptitude and attitude to be a successful rebreather diver.

- **Do you have the discipline to use the rebreather within the boundaries of its limitations?**

If you dive outside the boundaries of the capabilities of your rebreather you may be killed or seriously injured.

- **Do you have the discipline to use the rebreather within the boundaries of <u>your own</u> limitations?**

In most cases, rebreathers have more capability than you will be able to use safely. Making extended deep dives with a rebreather is extremely hazardous, even if you have all of the right back-up gear in place.

- **Do you have the discipline to know when it is safer not to dive?**

Some days, it's better not to get in the water. If you don't know when it's wiser to stay on the boat rather than going over the side, a rebreather is definitely not for you.

If you can't answer "yes" to all of the above questions, don't even contemplate purchasing a rebreather. If you still think you want a rebreather, we recommend taking a rebreather orientation course to see whether the experience matches your expectations.

IF YOU PURCHASE A REBREATHER

If you purchase a rebreather be sure to follow the procedures for use that you learn in your training course, as well as those recommended in the owner's manual. Perform the required maintenance religiously and keep your skills up to date. With a rebreather you can enjoy new and unique diving adventures, provided you give the equipment the respect it deserves.

Rebreather diving is fun!

ABOUT THE AUTHORS

Steve Barsky with his wife, Kristine, at Santa Cruz Island.
(© Bob Evans. La Mer Bleu Productions.)

STEVE BARSKY

Steve Barsky started diving in 1965 in Los Angeles County, and became a NAUI instructor in 1970. His first employment in the industry was with a dive store in Los Angeles and he went on to work for almost 10 years in the retail dive store environment.

Steve attended the University of California at Santa Barbara, where he earned a Master's Degree in 1976 in Human Factors Engineering. His degree has contributed to his thorough understanding of diving equipment design and use. His master's thesis was one of the first to deal with the use of underwater video systems in commercial diving. His work was a pioneering effort at the time (1976) and was used by the Navy in developing applications for underwater video systems.

His background includes being a commercial diver, working in the offshore oil industry in the North Sea, Gulf of Mexico, and South America. He worked as both an air diving supervisor and a mixed gas saturation diver, making working dives down to 580'.

Steve left the offshore aspects of commercial diving and went into the manufacturing end of the business in 1983. Barsky was marketing manager for Viking America, Inc., an international manufacturer of dry suits. He also served in a similar position at Diving Systems International (DSI), the world's leading manufacturer of commercial diving helmets. At DSI, Barsky worked very closely with Bev Morgan, a diving pioneer.

A prolific writer and professional underwater photographer, Barsky's articles have been published in *Sea Technology, Underwater USA, Skin Diver, Offshore Magazine, Emergency, Fire Engineering, Dive Training Magazine, Searchlines, Sources, Undersea Biomedical Reports, Santa Barbara Magazine, Selling Scuba, Scuba Times, Underwater Magazine*, and many other publications. He is the author of the *Dry Suit Diving Manual, Diving in High Risk Environments, Spearfishing for Skin and Scuba Divers, Small Boat Diving, Diving with the EXO-26 Full Face Mask, Diving with the Divator MK II Full Face Mask,* and a joint author with Dick Long and Bob Stinton of *Dry Suit Diving: A Guide to Diving Dry.* He is also a joint author of *Careers in Diving,* with his wife, Kristine and Ronnie Damico. Steve has taught numerous workshops on contaminated water diving, dry suits, small boat diving, spearfishing, and other diving topics.

In 1989 Steve formed Marine Marketing and Consulting, based in Santa Barbara, California. The company provides market research, marketing plans, consulting, newsletters, promotional articles, technical manuals, and other services for the diving and ocean industry. He has consulted to Dräger in Germany, U.S. Divers Co., Inc., Zeagle Systems, Inc., Diving Unlimited Intnl., Diving Systems Intnl, DAN, NAUI, and numerous other companies. He also investigates diving accidents and serves as an expert witness in dive accident litigation.

Steve has been an active rebreather diver since 1996 and is a NAUI and TDI rebreather diving instructor for the Dräger semi-closed circuit system.

MARK THURLOW

Mark Thurlow started diving in 1973 in high school and has worked as a diving professional ever since. Starting in retail sales at the Diving Locker Stores in San Diego, his career took him into professional diving where he has recovered 35 downed aircraft and numerous sunken boats.

In 1982, Mark started his own company, Hydra Marine, specializing in light construction, salvage and remotely operated vehicle operations. Mark's diving history includes working in the oceanographic/scientific field doing side scan surveys, biological assessments and hazardous materials sampling.

For the past 4 years Mark has been working in the film and television industry working with such noted filmmakers as; Howard Hall, Marty Snyderman and Al Giddings.

Mark Thurlow has been involved with numerous underwater film productions.

His list of film and TV credits include: the IMAX feature "The Living Sea", the first 3-D IMAX film "Into the Deep", Howard Halls' TV series "Secrets of the Ocean Realm", James Cameron's feature film "Titanic", Marty Snyderman's film "Sharks", and Al Giddings' TV production "Whales". In January 1998 Mark started another IMAX film with Howard Hall Productions which included six months of diving at Cocos Island.

In 1995, Mark got his first rebreather, a CCR 155. His teachers were Cmdr. Clark Presswood SEAL (Ret.) who specialized in underwater operations, rebreather research and training, as well as Howard Hall and Bob Cranston, both pioneers in using rebreathers in underwater filmmaking. Mark currently has over 250 logged hours on rebreathers and does much of the technical maintenance on his and the other filmmakers' rigs. They have over 1000 combined hours on these rigs with no major failures of any kind, a remarkable safety record.

Mark has been a consultant to Bio-Marine Industries and made the first dives with the new BMR 500 system, designed for the technical diver.

MIKE WARD

Mike Ward became a diving enthusiast in the mid 1960s by skin and scuba diving the lakes and quarries of Massachusetts and Maine.

Enlisting in the United States Navy in 1971, Mike served on nuclear submarines until completing Diver Second Class training in 1974. After a typical Second Class diver tour (i.e., lots of water time) aboard the U.S.S. Sunbird, ASR-15, Mike attended Diver First Class training (mixed gas) in 1977. He was ultimately assigned to the Navy Experimental Diving Unit, the world's premiere deep diving complex.

Mike Ward has tested numerous rebreather systems.

While attached to NEDU, Mike began his training in deep diving hyperbaric systems and qualified as a USN Saturation Diver. From 1977 until his retirement from the Navy in 1992, Mike served as a saturation diver and systems technician on virtually all USN deep diving assets. Much of his involvement with Navy diving included the test and evaluation of various underwater breathing apparatus (UBA) and support systems proposed for military use.

Mike has been trained in the use of numerous rebreather systems including the Dräger LAR V, the Spirotechnique Oxy-NG, the Bio-Marine CCR 1000, Fullerton-Sherwood's systems, and the Navy MK15, MK16, MK11, and MK12. He is knowledgeable regarding both closed circuit and semi-closed circuit systems.

Mike's insights into diving system design and fabrication led to his employment as a Senior Research Systems Analyst for Analysis and Technology, Inc., a defense contractor, where he was involved with the development of various recompression chamber and support van configurations for USN EOD and Marine Corps applications. He also authored technical publications for the Navy on various UBA, and assisted with the development of several diver propulsion vehicles for military combat swimmers. In 1997, Mike joined Diving Systems International, the Santa Barbara, California based manufacturer of commercial diving equipment, as their military liaison and as a new product prototype engineer.

An avid sport diver, Mike resides in Panama City Beach, Florida, with his wife Paula and sons, Mike Jr., and Steve.

GLOSSARY

Absorbent: A chemical compound designed to remove carbon dioxide from a mixture of gases. The primary ingredient in most absorbents is soda lime. As a result of its reaction with carbon dioxide, heat and moisture are normally produced as by-products.

Bail-out System: A back-up system used by divers in the event their primary gas supply fails. In the case of a rebreather diver, the system may include a completely redundant breathing system, or may depend on a diluent supply with a sufficient oxygen percentage to maintain consciousness at the surface and connected to an open circuit regulator.

Break-through Time: The amount of time that it takes for the absorbent in a particular canister to reach the point where it no longer effectively removes carbon dioxide. Once the level of carbon dioxide in the system exceeds .5% the break-through point has been reached.

Breathing Bag: A flexible bag that is part of the rebreather's breathing circuit that helps to reduce the surge in the breathing supply and serves as a reservoir for breathing gas. See also counterlung.

Breathing Loop: The low pressure circuit in a rebreather where the breathing gas circulates. The corrugated breathing hoses, breathing bags, and scrubber are all part of the breathing loop. This includes the air passages in the diver's body where air normally circulates during respiration.

Bypass Valve: A manual control valve that is used to add additional gas to the breathing loop.

Canister: The device in the breathing loop that holds the carbon dioxide absorbent. Also known as the scrubber or scrubber canister. Any of these terms is acceptable.

Carbon Dioxide: The waste product of respiration. Carbon dioxide also serves as the trigger for the body to breathe. It is toxic in high concentrations.

Caustic Cocktail: When a carbon dioxide absorbent accidentally mixes with water it produces a caustic solution that will "burn" your body. This is known as a caustic cocktail.

Counterlung: The breathing bags that are used in a rebreather may also be referred to as the counterlung.

Diluent: The gas used to "dilute" the pure oxygen in the breathing mixture. In most cases, the diluent will be air, or some other mixture that contains oxygen.

Fully Closed Circuit Rebreather: A rebreather where all of the diver's exhaled gas is recirculated through the system. Oxygen is added as needed and carbon dioxide is removed. No gas is lost except during an ascent when the gas expands and excess pressure must be vented off. Also referred to as a "CCR" or "rig".

Hypercapnia: A physiological condition that occurs when a person is exposed to a high level of carbon dioxide. More commonly referred to as carbon dioxide poisoning. The most striking symptom of hypercapnia is extreme shortness of breath.

Hyperoxia: A physiological condition that occurs when a diver is exposed to a high level (ppO$_2$) of oxygen. Individual susceptibility to hyperoxia varies widely, even among individuals on a day-to-day basis. The most serious symptom of hyperoxia is a convulsion and there is usually little or no advance warning.

Hypoxia: A physiological condition that occurs when a person is exposed to a breathing mixture that contains a very low level of oxygen. If the oxygen in a rebreather falls to a dangerously low level a diver can pass out without warning.

Molecular Sieve: A device that filters out carbon dioxide as gas passes through it. Although not perfected for rebreather diving, it offers promise as a replacement for scrubbers that use chemical absorbent.

Open Circuit Scuba: Traditional scuba gear that uses a demand regulator where every breath the diver takes is exhaled into the water.

Oxygen Sensor: An electro-chemical device that gives off an electrical voltage based on the amount of oxygen in a gas mixture.

ppCO$_2$: Shorthand method of denoting the partial pressure of carbon dioxide.

ppO$_2$: Shorthand method of denoting the partial pressure of oxygen.

Primary Display: A simple "idiot light" display used on most rebreathers to provide "at-a-glance" information on the status of the oxygen level in the rebreather.

Scrubber: The canister that holds the carbon dioxide absorbent in the rebreather.

Secondary Display: A more complex display that provides numerical readings on the level of oxygen in a rebreather.

Semi-Closed Circuit Rebreather: A type of breathing apparatus that recirculates some, but not all, of each breath of gas taken by the diver. Semi-closed circuit rebreathers are typically simpler and less expensive than fully closed circuit systems.

Set Point: The level at which the ppO_2 is set in a fully closed circuit electronic rebreather.

BIBLIOGRAPHY

Anonymous. *Safety and Handling Considerations* in <u>The Sodasorb Manual</u>, W.R. Grace, CT, 1993, pgs. S1-S6

Bove, A. and Wells, J. *Mixed Gas Diving.* in <u>Diving Medicine</u>. Bove, A. and Davis, J., editors. W. B. Saunders and Co., Philadelphia, PA. 1990. pgs. 50-58

Clarke, D.W. *The History of Breathing Apparatus and Current State of the Art* in <u>Lung Physiology and Divers' Breathing Apparatus</u>. Flook, V. and Brubakk, A. editors. Sintef Unimed, Gas Services, Seaway, University of Aberdeen. Aberdeen, Scotland. 1992. pgs. 125-146

Clarke, J. *Work of Breathing in Underwater Breathing Apparatus and CO2 Buildup* in <u>Proceedings of the Rebreather Forum 2.0</u>, Diving Science and Technology, Santa Ana, CA, 1996. pgs. P69-P75

Dewey and Almy Chemical Division. *HP Sodasorb Absorbent Characteristics: Underwater Diving Experiment* in <u>The Sodasorb Manual</u>, W.R. Grace, CT, 1993, pgs. 02-05

Dräger. *Atlantis I Mixed Gas Rebreather: Instructions for Use.* 2nd edition. Lubeck, Germany, 1996

Donald, K. *Oxygen and the Diver.* The SPA Ltd., Worcestshire, England. 1992. 237 pages

Elliott, D. *Safe Oxygen: How Low Can You Go?* in <u>Proceedings of the Rebreather Forum 2.0</u>, Diving Science and Technology, Santa Ana, CA, 1996. pgs. P19-P22

Jackson, P. *The Fleuss Apparatus - A Short History of the Rebreather.* Unpublished manuscript, 1996

Kemp, P. *Underwater Warriors.* Naval Institute Press, Annapolis, Maryland. 1996. 256 pages

Luchtenberg, D. *Nitrox Rebreather Manual: A Manual of Training Methods in the Use of Semi-Closed Circuit Rebreather.* Rebreather Advisory Board. Konstanz, Germany, 1996. 210 pages

U.S. Navy. *Operation and Maintenance Instructions: Underwater Breathing Apparatus, MK15 Mod 0*, Naval Sea Systems Command, Washington, D.C. 1982

Nuckols, M., Tucker, W., Sarich, A. *Life Support Systems Design.* Simon and Schuster Custom Publishing, Needham Heights, MA, 1996. 295 pages

Ornhagen, H. and Loncar, M. *Lab Testing Today's Rebreathers* in <u>Proceedings of the Rebreather Forum 2.0</u>, Diving Science and Technology, Santa Ana, CA, 1996. pgs. P9-P14

Palmer, R. and Hamilton, W. *Nitrox Semi-Closed Circuit Rebreather Manual.* Technical Diving International, Bath, Maine. 1995

Rexnord. *CCR 155 Operation Manual.* Rexnord, Malvern, PA. Undated

Starck, W. *Electrolung*. in <u>AquaCorps Journal</u>. Key West, FL. Vol. 7. December, 1993. pgs. 6, 8

Stolp, B., and Moon, R. *Physiological Factors in Carbon Dioxide Removal* in <u>The Sodasorb Manual</u>, W.R. Grace, CT, 1993, pgs. M6-M16

Stolp, B., and Moon, R. *Soda Lime Reactivity* in <u>The Sodasorb Manual</u>, W.R. Grace, CT, 1993, pgs. M17-M20

Thalmann, E. *Evaluating Rebreather Performance* in <u>Proceedings of the Rebreather Forum 2.0</u>, Diving Science and Technology, Santa Ana, CA, 1996. pgs. P31-P36

Thalmann, E. *Rebreather Basics* in <u>Proceedings of the Rebreather Forum 2.0</u>, Diving Science and Technology, Santa Ana, CA, 1996. pgs. P23-P29

Thom, S. and Clark, J. *The Toxicity of Oxygen, Carbon Monoxide, and Carbon Dioxide* in <u>Diving Medicine</u>. Bove, A. and Davis, J., editors. W. B. Saunders and Co., Philadelphia, PA. 1990. pgs. 82-94

U.S. Navy. *U.S. Navy Diving Manual*, Volume 2, Mixed-Gas Diving. Best Publishing Co., Flagstaff, AZ. 1991

INDEX

Abalone rig 20
Absorbent 55, 82, 104, 135, 181
Absorbent dust 49, 104, 162
Absorbent efficiency 81
Absorbent failure 134
Air . . . . 31, , 149, 168
Air diving table 122, 196
Air hose 12
Air hunger 179
Alarm 68
Alarm light 178
Alkali 12
Anchor line 157
Aqualung® Group 21
Ascent 78, 129, 149, 177
Asphyxia 82
Atmospheric pressure 199
Audio alarms 30

Back mounted breathing bags 60
Back mounted buoyancy
    compensators 159
Back mounted rebreather
    systems 194
Back-up dive computer 196
Bacteria 38, 137, 186
Baffle 57
Baffle system 59, 83, 133
Baggage allowance 41
Baggage fees 155
Bail-out 33, 79, 92-93, 109
    . . . . 132, 134, 180, 195

Bail-out bottle 35, 62, 92-95
    . . . . 109, 123, 129, 158-159
Bail-out regulator 36
Bail-out system 23, 68, 75, 92, 125
    . . . . 128, 134, 160, 193
Battery 5, 8, 36, 54, 68
    . . . . 140-141, 147, 153-154
    . . . . 163-164, 177, 198
Battery housing 164
Battery life 68, 177
Beach 135
Beckman Instruments 17
Betadine 187
Biologically polluted water 189
Bio-Marine BMR500 . . . . 5, 18, 35
    . . . . 84, 144, 158
Bio-Marine CCR155 144
Boat 135
Boat captain 157
Boat owner 201
Body temperature 29
Bottom time 27, 86, 121, 140, 148
Breakthrough point 50, 81
Breakthrough time 81
Breathing bag 2-3, 23, 36, 40, 45
    . . . . . 58-59, 60, 62, 76, 88, 101-103
    . . . . 107, 114, 119, 127, 129
    . . . . . . 130-131, 134, 137, 144, 186
Breathing gas 65, 92, 126
Breathing hose failure 39
Breathing hoses 2, 23, 36, 45
    . . . . 67, 95-96, 108, 170
Breathing loop 86, 128, 144
    . . . . 147, 177, 182, 186

Breathing medium 36
Breathing resistance 62, 64, 97, 133
Breathlessness. 75, 79
Bubbles. . . . 1, 30, 43, 89, 152, 156, 171
Buddy 98, 131, 170, 172, 179
Buddy check. 170
Buoyancy 23, 94, 97, 130, 176
Buoyancy compensator 23, 35, 62
. . . . . 92, 95, 125, 127, 129, 159, 199
Buoyancy control 68, 93, 140
Burst disk 175, 184
Bypass (demand valve). 108
Bypass controls. 172
Bypass valve 30, 86, 88, 146, 177

Cables 171
Calcium hydroxide. 48
Calibration procedure 166
California Department of
 Fish and Game 43
Canister. 49, 51-53, 59, 73
 . . . . 80-81, 133-134
Canister breakthrough time 46
Canister duration 68
Canvas 58
Carbon dioxide. 1, 11, 13, 50, 54
 . . . . 73, 79, 81-82, 105, 133-134
 . . . . 147, 179-180, 191
Carbon dioxide "scrubber" 2
Carbon dioxide absorbent 4, 23, 33
 . . . . 35-36, 41, 48, 90, 134, 152-153
Carbon dioxide build-up 105
Carbon dioxide poisoning . . . 39, 70, 79
Carlton Industries 18
Caustic chemicals. 39, 195
Caustic cocktail 83, 106, 133, 174
Caustic soda 48, 82
Cave divers. 140, 159
CCR. 139-142, 144, 148, 149
 . . . . 151-152, 154-156, 160-161
 . . . 166-168, 172, 174, 176, 179, 181
CCR 155 . . . . 158, 178
CE certification. 47
CE testing. 47
CE mark 46
Center of buoyancy 46
Channeling 80, 104-105
Check valves. 30
Checklist. 107, 154
Chemical absorbent 55, 59, 105

Chemical burns 70, 80, 106, 133
Chemical indicator. 105
Chemical reaction 52
Chest 59
Chest mounted breathing bags. 60
Christolube. 156
Cis-Lunar 5, 34, 43, 144, 159, 180
Closed circuit mixed gas rebreathers . . 5
Closed circuit oxygen rebreather 15
Clumping 53
CNS convulsion 118
CNS level of oxygen 98, 119, 136
CNS oxygen exposure . . . 118, 120, 122
CNS oxygen exposure tables 120
CNS oxygen toxicity. 179
CO_2. . . . . 79-80, 83, 128
CO_2 absorbent 81, 155, 181, 187-188
Cobra 4
Cold water 33
Color indicator. 52
Color reversion. 53
Communications 101
Compressed air 39-40, 69
Compressed air scuba. 2
Compressor 201
Computer interface 68
Condensation 172, 174
Consciousness 101
Consumable items 155, 202
Convulsions 72
Corrosion 110
Corrugated hose 64, 96
Corrugations. 186
Cough. 181
Counter lung 23, 144
Counter weights. 174
Cousteau, Jacques. 11
Craig, John D. 16
Crossover point 149, 151
Cryogenics 54
Current. 101
Cut-off depth. 100, 117-118
Cylinder 78, 88, 90, 99-100
 . . . . 103, 107-108, 121-122
 . . . . 125, 135, 146, 155
Cylinder valve 115, 125, 172

Dangers. 69
Dealer support 65
Death 70, 132

Decompression 1, 39, 84, 119-120
. . . 122, 144, 148-149, 151, 159, 183
Decompression limits. 168
Decompression calculations. 8, 21
Decompression dive 32, 85
. . . . 169, 172, 196
Decompression information. 196
Decompression obligation . 39, 117, 119
Decompression sickness. 28, 32, 70
. . . . 94, 102, 110, 129, 131, 196
Decompression status. 98, 146
Decompression stops 151
Deep diving 32
Dehydration 28
Demand valve. 86, 88, 107, 109
. . . . 126, 128
Depth capability 5
Depth gauge 1
Depth limitations 4, 142
Depth range 98
Descent. 88, 142
Desco (Diving Equipment Supply
  Company). 16
Desiccant pack 186
Diaphragm 165
Diffuser. 30
Diluent 33, 48, 90, 103, 144
. . . . 146-147, 149, 151, 155, 159-160
. . . . 164, 168, 171, 174-175, 178
. . . . 180, 184
Diluent addition valve 165
Diluent bypass valve. 164
Diluent cylinder 164
Discipline 201, 204
Disinfectants. 34, 137, 187, 189
Disinfection 186
Displays 146
Dive boat 8, 156
Dive computer 33, 46, 98, 110, 117
. . . . 119–122, 125, 152, 169
. . . . 189, 195-196
Dive partner 125
Dive planning. 39, 117
Dive profile. 157
Dive shop 141
Dive time 103
Dive trip 98, 104
Divemaster® 157
Divesorb® 48, 52
Diving Equipment Manufacturer's
  Association (DEMA) 20

Diving professional. 140
Dizziness. 72, 75
Doctor. 106
Donald, Dr. Kenneth 73
Dräger. 4, 15, 20, 48, 57, 78
. . . . 82, 99, 101, 110
Dräger Atlantis I 30, 35-36
Dräger, Dr. Bernhard 13
Dräger LAR V 43, 51
Drop cloth 104
Drowning 70, 189
Dry mouth 1
Dry suit. 25, 33, 92, 127, 129
Drying cabinet 38, 137
Drysuit 182
Dump valve 148
Dwell 50

Ead. 168
Efficiency 27
Electric motors 138
Electrolung. 17
Electrolyte 199
Electronic control. 178
Electronic failure 39
Electronic wireless system 189
Electronics 3, 5, 62, 74, 119
. . . . . . 135, 141, 144, 146-147, 154
. . . . 164-165, 167, 178, 189
Electronics failure 147, 154
Emergency 132, 174
Emergency ascent. 78
Emergency procedures 153-154
. . . . 172, 181
Entanglement 93
EOBA 20, 22
Equalizing device 191
Equipment 36
Equivalent air depth 151, 168
Ergonomics. 46
Esophagus 83
Exercise 73
Exertion level 184
Exhalation. 61-62, 90, 97, 133
Exhalation bag 59, 89
Exhalation hose 173
Exhalation pressure 123
Exhalation valve 108, 161
Exhaled breath 174
Exhaust. 30

Exhaust valve 90, 97, 115-116
. . . . 123, 130, 133, 166, 176
Extended deep dives. 204
Eye protection 49, 162
Eyes. 190, 194-195

Failure. 193
Fatal accident 39, 128
Fatigue 29, 179
Feedback line 90
Fenzy P-68 22
Fiberglass 62
Fieno. 35
Filters 83
First stage 86, 113
Fit. 190
Fittings. 123, 168
Fleuss, Henry 12-13
Fleuss Mask 12
Flow check. 77
Flow rate 107, 113, 121-122
Flow test. 109
Flying a rig 167
Foam padding. 155
Forced air circulation. 137
Frame. 191
Free radical intermediates 71
Freezing temperatures 81
Fresh water. 185
Fuel cell 147, 198
Full face mask. 71-72, 74, 148
. . . . 189-190, 192-194
Fully closed circuit electronic
    rebreather. 32, 34, 66, 74
Fully closed circuit mixed gas
    rebreather. 2-3, 139, 152
Fully closed circuit oxygen
    rebreathers 3
Fully closed circuit rebreather 1, 25
. . . . 39, 70, 148-149, 170, 174
Fully closed circuit system. . . 30, 71, 85
Fungus 38, 186

Gagnan, Emil 11
Gas consumption 196
Gas cylinders 2
Gas mixture 74, 99, 101, 103, 107
Gas supply 192
Gloves. 49, 63, 162

Government agencies. 4, 66
Grand Bleu 9
Grand mal seizure 72

Hall, Howard. . . . . : 18
Harbors. 190
Hard wire communications 25
Harness. 95
Hass, Hans 15
Hass, Lotte 15
Hazards 69-70
Head 173
Headache 79, 179
Heat 83
Heavy work loads. 99
Heliox. 36, 41, 48, 86, 90, 125
. . . . 142, 144, 146, 159, 168
Helium 5, 27, 34, 41
Helmet 101
High Performance Sodasorb® 48
High pressure hose. 175
High work load. 101
Hood. 191
Horse collar BC 159
Hose clamps 93
Hoseless dive computer 196
Hoses. 134, 152, 163, 181, 186-187
Hospital 70
Hot water heaters 138
Human factors testing 45
Hypercapnia 70, 79, 179-180
. . . . 184, 187
Hyperoxia. 70
Hypothermia. 29, 50
Hypoxia. 39, 70, 75, 77-79, 110
. . . . . . 125, 128, 130, 175, 177, 179
Hypoxic mix. 175

Ice 81
Impact resistant plastic. 191
Inert gas 5, 33
Inflatable. 104
Inhalation 60, 62, 88
Inhalation bag . . 59, 78, 89-90, 101, 118
Inhalation valve 108, 161
Injector blockage 39
Inlet valve. 63
Inspired percentage of oxygen 121
Instructor 47, 95
Insulin 73

Insulin dependent diabetic 73
Intelligibility 192
Intermediate pressure 113
Inventors 45
Irrigation canals 190
Irritability 72
ISO 9000 46

Jaw 194

Kanwisher, John 17
Kelp 93

LAR V 5
Law enforcement agencies 43
Leak 113-114, 116-117
. . . . 126, 165, 172, 181
Leak test 114, 166, 185
Lens 191, 193
Lever 63, 114, 132-133, 193, 195
Lexan® 191
Lid 106
Life-support system 11, 141
Lime 48, 83
Linear scrubber 57
Lips 83, 106
Liquid chemical catalysts 23
Lithium hydroxide 48, 83
Logbook 113, 141-142, 154, 187
Loop 88, 175, 187
Loop volume 166
Loss of buoyancy 133
Low pressure hose 92
Low temperatures 81
Lower back 174
Lubricants 34, 48, 156
Lung capacity 58
Lung over-pressure accident 70, 72
Lung volume 97
Lungs 83, 88, 106
Lysol IC Quaternary cleaner . . . 186-187

M-15 193-194
Maintenance 36, 142, 178
. . . . 185, 201, 204
Manual 65
Manual control 178

Manufacturer 65, 107, 110
Manufacturer's repair course 65
Margin of safety 170
Marine biologist 15
Marine life injuries 70
Mask 88, 128, 172
Mask straps 191
Mass flow systems 85
Material Safety Data Sheet (MSDS) . 155
Maximum depth 67, 100, 168
Maximum dive time 68
McKenny, John 18
Mechanical aptitude 203
Medical grade oxygen 4, 33, 156
Mesh size 53, 68
Metered orifice 76, 86, 88, 90
. . . . 98, 108, 110, 113, 121-122
Microprocessor 21, 144
Military 101
Military divers 3, 17
Military operations 4, 30
Mini-Lung 17
Mix 94, 128
Mixed gas diving 201
MK 15 178
MK 16 18
Moisture 28, 50, 56, 83, 135
Moisture absorbers 162
Molecular Products 49
Molecular sieve 54
Morgan, Bev 19
Morgan Diving Corporation 193
Mouth 83, 106, 131, 190, 194
Mouth pod 193
Mouthpiece 2, 35, 63, 72, 79, 89
. . . . . 95-96, 108, 114, 117, 131, 135
. . . 138, 147, 161, 163, 165, 171, 173,
. . . . 180-181, 189-190, 195
Mouthpiece mounting tube 190
MSA (Mine Safety Apparatus) 16
MSDS (Material Safety Data Sheet) . . 49
Multi-level dive 169
Multimeter 163

Nausea 72
Navy Experimental Diving Unit 46
Navy MK11 Mod 0 19
Negative pressure leak test 109
Neutrally buoyant 174
Nitrogen 1-2, 5, 142, 149, 151, 183

Nitrogen elimination 151
Nitrogen narcosis 70, 151
Nitrox 7-8, 21, 27-28, 31, 36
. . . . 41, 48, 77, 86, 88, 94, 99
. . . . . . 103, 113, 118, 121-122, 126
. . . . . . 131, 136, 142, 167, 196, 201
Nitrox computer 168-169
Nitrox dive tables 110
Nitrox tag 103
Nitrox training 153
No-decompression 149
No-decompression dives 85
No-decompression limits . . 99-100, 121
No-decompression time 117
Noise 127
Non-return valve 107-108
Nose 88, 128, 130, 148
. . . . 172, 182-184, 190, 194-195
Numbness in the lips 75

O-ring 153, 156, 163, 175, 184
O$_2$ grease 153
O$_2$ pressure gauge 175
O$_2$ sensor wires 163
Ocean Technology Systems 192
Octopus rig 92
Odor 187
One-way valves 89, 147, 161
Open circuit nitrox 31
Open circuit nitrox 31
Open circuit scuba 5, 17, 25
. . . . 28, 33, 35, 37, 43, 75
. . . . 99, 125, 136, 161, 185, 202
Open circuit second stage 92
Operating costs 33
Operational depth 67
Optical qualities 191
Oral/nasal mask 191
Owner's manual 68, 109, 113
. . . . 134, 136
Oxy-NG 21
Oxygen 1-5, 8, 12, 31, 41
. . . . 47, 68, 71, 74, 77-78, 82
. . . . . . 88, 90, 98-103, 110, 117-121
. . . . 125, 142, 144, 146, 149
. . . . . . 152, 156, 160, 163-166, 168
. . . . 171, 176-178, 182-184, 198
Oxygen analyzer . . 34, 36, 168, 189, 198
Oxygen bypass valve 165
Oxygen consumption 77-78

. . . . 100-102, 122
Oxygen convulsion 71, 75, 99
Oxygen cylinder 165
Oxygen cylinder valve 178
Oxygen exposure time 73
Oxygen monitoring 118
Oxygen monitoring system 8, 68
. . . . 79, 135
Oxygen partial pressure 27
Oxygen percentage 75, 103
Oxygen seizure 128
Oxygen sensor 5, 23, 46, 76, 117
. . . . . . 141, 144, 147, 153, 163, 186
Oxygen supply 184
Oxygen supply valve 176
Oxygen toxicity . . 39, 69-72, 74, 79, 128
Oxygen uptake 77
Oxylighte 13

Partial pressure . . 21, 31, 70-71, 74, 78
. . . . 99, 118, 140, 142, 146-147, 201
Percentage of oxygen 168-169
Personal injury 83, 116
Physical dimensions 67
Physical hazards 151
Physician 84
Physiological risks 38, 69
Plastic 62
Pneumatics 144, 146
Pockets 95
Polluted waters 43
Positive pressure leak test 115-116
Post dive maintenance 37, 141, 202
Potassium hydroxide 48
Power inflator 92, 95, 129
Power switch 166
ppCO$_2$ 184
ppO$_2$ 70-71, 74, 99-100, 118
. . . . 128-130, 142-144, 146-147, 149
. . . . 151, 163, 168-169, 171-172
. . . . 175-178, 182, 184, 196
ppO$_2$ setpoint 168
Pre-dive checklist 175
Pre-dive flow check 76
Pre-dive prep 33, 142, 160, 167
Pre-mixed gas 103
Precautionary decompression
stop 94, 129, 131-132, 134, 183
Pressure gauge 45, 146, 184
Pressure gradient 54

Primary display 146, 164, 172
. . . . 175, 177-178
Principle of operation. 67
Prism Topaz 5, 34, 144, 163, 185
Proportioning system 85
Public safety divers. 43
Pulmonary oxygen toxicity 70
Purge 88
Purge button. 194
Puritan Bennett. 49
Pyle, Richard 42

Readey, Peter 10-11
Radial scrubber. 57
Rebreather. 91-92, 101, 107, 113
. . . . 115, 117, 123, 125-126
. . . . 128, 130, 139, 154-155
. . . . . . 157, 178, 185, 189-190, 202
Rebreather failure. 39, 132
Rebreather manufacturers 169
Rebreather orientation course 204
Rebreather system flood. 195
Rebreather training course 66
Recreational diver. 21, 85
Recreational diving 5, 7-8, 11, 17
Regeneration. 53
Regulator 2, 35, 45, 47, 86, 88
. . . . 90, 109, 123, 146, 181, 194
Regulator failure. 39
Regulator noise. 140
Remaining bottom time 196
Resistance to breathing 180
Restrictor 199
Retractors 158
Rig 85, 139, 165-166, 170-171
. . . . 180, 182, 187
Rigging 157
Ringing of the ears 72
Risk. 39, 69, 84
Rolleimarin camera 15
Royal British Navy 73
Rubber gloves. 199

Safe handling procedures 49
Safety factor 32, 196
Safety precautions 69
Safety stop 157
Saliva 135, 172
Salt water 59

Scientific diving 42
Scrubber 23, 55, 58-59, 62
. . . . 68, 73, 81, 89-90, 105, 135
. . . . 144, 147, 180-181, 187-188
Scrubber crash 184, 187
Scrubber canister 36, 45, 79, 82
. . . 101, 103-104, 106-107, 114, 162
Scrubber leakage. 39
Scrubber performance 56
Scrubber reaction 174
Scuba 69
Scuba cylinders. 34
Scuba mask 192-193
Scubapro's Air II. 92
Seal 190
Search and rescue divers 190
Search and rescue diving 42
Seats 48
Second stage 109
Secondary display. 146, 165, 170
. . . . 172, 176-178, 182, 184
Self-discipline 154
Self-mixing system 103
Semi-closed circuit rebreather
. . . . 3, 7-8, 19, 21, 25, 30
. . . . 32, 34, 69, 71, 76-77
. . . . 85-86, 99, 101, 113
. . . . . . 118-119, 129, 135, 148, 174
Semi-closed mode. 184
Semi-permeable membranes. 54
Setpoint 147, 151, 172
Shake test 162
Shallow water diving 94
Shortness of breath. 82
Shoulder 60, 62
Shroud 62, 107, 171
Siebe-Gorman. 13
Silica gel 186
Sinus squeeze 70
Skills. 204
Skin. 106
Small boat. 41, 104
Snorkel 98, 192-193
Snyderman, Marty 18
Soda lime. 48, 50, 54, 82-83, 181
Sodasorb® 52
Sodium hydroxide 48
Sofnolime® 49
Solenoid 153, 178
Solenoid addition valves. 30
. . . . 146-147, 176

Spacer 162
Spare parts 65, 152
Special tools 65
Spirotechnique 4, 21
Sport diving market 5
Standardization. 63
Starck, Walter. 17
Steam Machines, Inc. 5, 10, 159
Stelzner, Hermann 15
Stiffeners. 64
Storage 38
Submersible pressure gauge . . . 125-126
Sun 136
Sunlight 59, 137
Super coolants 54
Surface 78
Surface interval. 136
Surface supplied diving gear 25
Surface swimming 98
Symptoms. 75

Tabata's Duo-Air 92
Tactical diving 43
Tarp 104
Task loading. 40
Technical diver. 5, 42
Technical diving. 3
Technician 113
Test apparatus 110
Test data 68
Test dives 66
Testing laboratories 66
Thermal protection 33, 152
Tidal volume 123
Time 1
Tools. 153
Training 41, 151, 153, 203
Travel 155
Trimix 27-28, 36, 142, 144
. . . . 146, 159, 168
Trouble shooting 153

Tunnel vision 75
Twitching of the lips 72

U.S. Divers Co., Inc. 21
U.S. Fish and Wildlife Service 43
U.S. Navy 5, 18
U.S. Navy Experimental Diving Unit
(NEDU) 45
Umbilical 101
Unconsciousness 75, 82
Undersea Technologies 5, 144
Underwater photographer 42
. . . . 140, 201
Underwater photography 40
User manual 46

Valve 63, 79, 88, 173
VENTID 72
Vibration. 105, 123
Vision distortion. 75
Visual disturbances 72
Volume. 191
Volume of oxygen 121

W.R. Grace 48
Warranty 65, 68
Water 63, 72, 80, 84, 132
. . . . 172, 180, 190
Water inhalation. 189
Water temperature 56
Weight. 65, 95-96, 174
Westinghouse. 17
Wetsuit. 25
Windpipe 83
Work load. 68, 100
Work of breathing 46
Working depth 103
Wreck divers 140, 159, 169

Zeagle Systems 160